ONE MAN'S FOREST

For Dick and Jim, who "taught us all we knew," but most specially for my wife Isabel, without whose help and joyful companionship all this would never have happened.

One Man's Forest

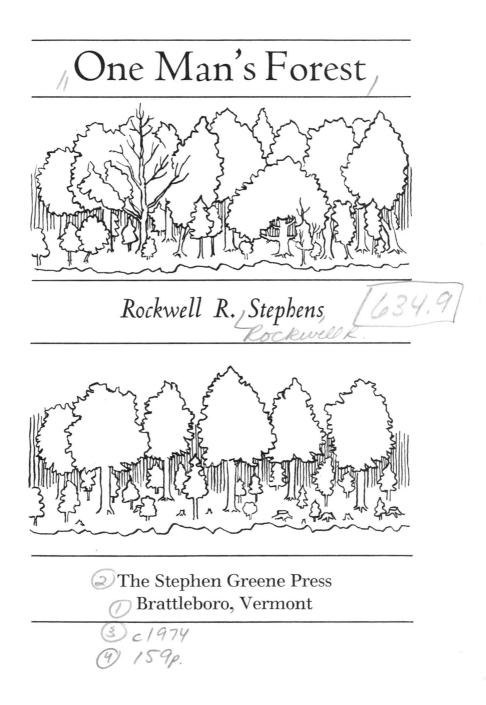

Rockwell R. Stephens

The Stephen Greene Press
Brattleboro, Vermont

The poem on page 87 is from *Winter in Vermont*, by Charles Edward Crane, copyright 1941 Alfred A. Knopf, Inc. Used by permission of the publisher.

The drawings in this book are by Walter Richardson, and Number 3 is based on "Forest Plantation Management," Bulletin of the Pennsylvania Dept. of Forests and Waters (1958), as reprinted in *Woodlands for Profit and Pleasure* by Reginald D. Forbes. Grateful acknowledgment is also made to the following photographers for their pictures used in this book: Robert Mertens for Nos. 2, 4, 5, 7, 8, 27, 33 and 34; Edward P. Lincoln for Nos. 13 and 18; Kathy Putnam for Nos. 20, 31 and 32; and George Schuler for Number 22.

This book has been produced in the United States of America: designed by R. L. Dothard Associates, composed by American Book–Stratford Press, and printed and bound by The Colonial Press. It is published by The Stephen Greene Press, Brattleboro, Vermont 05301.

Library of Congress Cataloging in Publication Data
Stephens, Rockwell R
    One man's forest.
    1. Wood-lots. I. Title.
SD387.W6S74   634.9′99   74–23687
ISBN 0–8289–0224–0
ISBN 0–8289–0225–9 pbk.

74 75 76 77 78 79 9 8 7 6 5 4 3 2 1

Contents

Preface

This is an attempt to tell something about what one does to make a modest-sized piece of woodland into a respectable bit of productive forest. And how a city bred couple, starting in their sixties some ten years ago, went about it. It is a personal narrative rather than a text book on forestry and logging, but the general principles as well as the specific procedures we followed are sufficiently detailed to serve as a "how to" guide for any ambitious amateur.

The precepts we followed were given us principally by our county forester, as well as by a friend who is an ecologist and conservationist of the first rank, and whose own woodlands under his intensive cultivation and management are a shining example of what an individual can accomplish.

This account of our adventures in forestry may, we hope, encourage others to take a greater and perhaps more informed interest in their own woodlands, and savor the pleasure we have derived from working in ours.

October 1973   ROCKWELL R. STEPHENS

I. Man Meets Woods

HOW A RETIRED CITY COUPLE
BECAME WOODLOTTERS

THE LOADING BOOM of the big logging truck picked up another sixteen-foot ash log and dropped it neatly on top of the load. "Must have nearly 3000 feet on by now, and that's enough," the driver said as he climbed down from his high seat on the loader. "We better chain up and get to the mill."

"Madam," I said as I turned to my wife, "do you realize this is a historic occasion?" For these were our own logs, felled by my hand, trimmed by hers, and brought out of the woods in a joint enterprise by a city-bred couple in their sixties who for most of their lives had known a forest only as scenery. That truck load of logs marked completion of a full cycle of woodlot cultivation, from primary steps to the ultimate objective of a log sale. It marked a high point in an avocation in which we had found many hours of new pleasures and satisfactions.

"What do you do, now that you have retired to the country," our metropolitan friends would ask. "We cultivate our woodlot," became a standard reply. We might add in further explanation, "We backed into amateur forestry through the woodshed." Even a confirmed city dweller recognizes the virtue of a supply of firewood.

Backing into forestry was no part of our ambition when we settled into a village in east central Vermont after a sampling of semirural living that we found wholly satisfying. The rolling hills and scattered farmlands around us were invitations to exploration by back road Jeeping and winter roaming on our cross country skis. Inevitably, we wanted a piece of this land to be ours. Ours to supply a little firewood perhaps, but more importantly, ours to roam and explore, to share with our children and grandchildren as we learned its intimacies, and perhaps most precious of all, a retreat to find the refreshment of a solitude free from man and all his noisy works.

We were fortunate beyond all expectation to find more than a hundred acres of hill, pasture and woodland which met our every aspiration. It is touched at one corner by a town road, little used but guaranteeing easy access the year around. Changing times had taken the open land out of farm cultivation more than a generation ago. An ambitious project with beef cattle had failed for lack of adequate pasturage on its depleted soil. Some eighty acres of woodland, rising several hundred feet above the open fields in irregular hilltops, had been cut over in a selective logging thirty years before.

It was a delight to explore the mixed hard- and softwood growth of straight and tall maple, beech and ash that had been mere saplings at the time of that earlier harvest. Hemlock stood along the brook. There was birch and much poplar. Several areas of long abandoned pasture were growing promising stands of young white pine.

But even our untutored eyes could detect evidence of wasteful growth and neglect. Any observer can

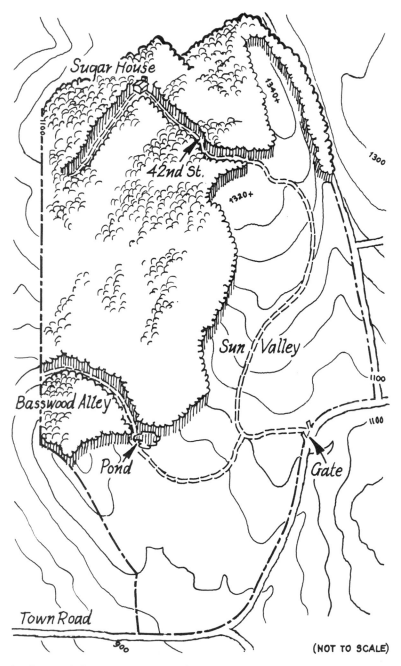

Sugar House

1340+

1300

42nd St.

1320+

Sun Valley

1100

Basswood Alley

1100

Pond

Gate

Town Road

900

(NOT TO SCALE)

1. Some eighty acres of woodland . . . had been cut over in a
   selective logging thirty years before.

recognize an untended, weed-grown garden. But our many acres of woodland would call for more than hoe and spading fork. Garden weeds are recognizable enough, and thinning a row of carrots needs little experience. But what were our forest weeds, and where and how much should one pluck from a woodlot? We needed the guidance of a professionally qualified forester.

No difficulty here. A call to our county forester brought immediate response and revealed the thoroughness with which state and federal agencies are prepared to meet the problems of the small landowner.

The Soil Conservation Service of the Department of Agriculture will prepare a land-use capability map on an aerial photograph. Soil types and topography are identified to indicate appropriate land use such as cropland, hay, woodland, or tree plantations. Regional staffs are usually headquartered in each county seat. Vermont was the first state to establish a professional forester in every county to advise any woodland owner and make available the specialists in the state department of forestry for consultation on many critical aspects of forestry practice. Through state and federal funding all these services are supplied at no cost to the individual landowner.

First step with our county forester was a tour of the woodlot to identify boundaries and to gain an impression of the general nature of what it contained. Next came the question "What do you want to do with it?" Our answer was "Everything"—and then, "Enjoy it." As it has turned out after some ten years, we have achieved a good measure of both objectives.

"Everything" is a large order. But there is an old nursery rhyme or saying—something about "how do you carve an elephant?" And the answer is, "Bit by bit." So it proved for this pair of elderly amateurs. Cultivating a woodlot has a basic similarity to cultivating a garden: keep down the weeds or hoe them out, thin the rows to give everything a share of growing room and sun, and harvest when full grown and ripe. But the garden is a seasonal enterprise running on a firm time schedule. Pick the peas and the beans right now—to-day or tomorrow, before they grow old and tough. The same with lettuce, and the tomato must come off the vine before it softens or rots.

A tree, on the other hand, may take sixty years to mature, and ten years or more before it needs much attention. The life cycle of a stand of maple may cover a full century. The time clock of the garden ticks in minutes. The woodland ticks in years.

It is a tribute to our forester's perception and skill that he tailored a program of Timber Stand Improvement (TSI, to use the technical abbreviation) to fit the aspirations of an amateur couple in their sixties and yet meet the standards of good forestry. "Bit by bit" became the basis of our operations, keyed to a flexible rule of first things first and paced to the extent of our time, energy, and developing skills. Thus ten- and later five-acre plots in the hardwoods became the order of business for several years. The forester in each case identified the trees to be cut in the course of weeding and thinning and inspected

our work when completed before outlining the next
project.

Our piecemeal process differs from the frequent
approach to a forest management program that begins with a complete timber cruise. Measured areas
are laid out and their contents identified and counted,
tree by tree, by size and species. This is, of course,
best done by a professional forester, but the process
is thoroughly described in forestry handbooks and is
not beyond the ability of an ambitious amateur.

Such a cruise may be necessary if a woodlot contains enough mature trees to warrant a timber sale.
It was our impression, however, later confirmed by
the forester, that we had comparatively few trees of
an age and size to require immediate harvesting and
sale. The largest of these had been promising young
growth when the area was cut over many years ago.
A far greater number of ash, beech, and maple now
were six to eight inches in diameter, tall and straight,
and overtopping many even younger trees, all competing for light and growing room. Let's get the
weeds out, we thought, do some thinning, and then
perhaps start counting our assets.

At any rate, we felt that we knew our woodlot
by the time, in early December, when our forester
gave us our first assignment for "weed and thin." We
had acquired our land in early summer. It had become so much of our everyday habitation that we
had already adopted place names to identify many
areas. How else to report that we watched a big dog
fox trot up through Sun Valley toward the Saffron
tree and turn down 42nd Street? That we would meet

2. Sun and snow make winter a beautiful time in the woods.

at noon at Banshee Gate, or that we would soon need a bridge on Basswood Alley to get over the brook?

Only one area contained anything of such size and age that immediate harvesting might be desirable. A number of old hemlocks stood in a grove, part of which was in our neighbor's woodland. In the course of checking our mutual boundary one day, he had remarked that the largest of these were nearly at an age beyond which decay would make them unsuitable for lumber.

As luck would have it we heard soon after that another neighbor needed three-inch planks for a bridge he was repairing, and wanted hemlock for its resistance to the weather. Here was just the customer we needed. A sale was soon negotiated. But we had no equipment to handle this enterprise. Our

chain saw was too small to tackle these monster trees
and we had no way to get them out of the woods.
But our little community proved to be rich in resources.

The neighbor whose woodlot abutted ours was the
very man who had logged over our property years
ago. His avocation was the raising and training of
oxen. "Won my first blue ribbon when I was fourteen," he once told us. A friend of his had a heavy
logging truck. A nearby farmer operated a small saw-
mill as a part time project. Our problems found instant solutions.

We had an exciting and instructive day watching
every detail of the felling and handling of those big
hemlocks. "Don't much like cutting these," our neighbor said as he readied his chain saw. "Old hemlock
like this, they get brashy and brittle and you can't
always be sure they're going to go the way you want
'em." And sure enough, one did go astray and fall
into the branches of another. We learned much from
the way he extricated a log from that situation, and
it was some solace, on later occasions when we would
hang a tree, to remember that even an old timer
could run into trouble.

There were other dividends from this enterprise to
enrich our experience and lend confidence to future
projects. We were to call on the irresistible power of
his big oxen some time later when neither our little
tractor nor the faithful Jeep could handle some big
logs felled in our first harvest of mature hardwoods.

The hemlock transaction and several later sales of
poplar were tangible evidence that our woodlot enter-

prise could be something more than just a pleasant avocation for a couple who liked to work in the woods. Our days of shared enterprise gave a rich store of satisfaction, but we nevertheless occasionally speculated about the validity of the whole undertaking. We could produce a few logs, a few cords of poplar, firewood for our own hearth—and a bit of improved woodland that would show as a mere dot on the millions of forest acres. Was all this just fun and games in the woods?

An overview of our national forest resources gives some perspective to the role of the small woodlotter. More than half—nearly 60 per cent, in fact—of all forest lands are in the hands of farmers and other private owners. Yet these lands produce less than half our wood products. For lack of management these acres are producing no more than a third to a half of what they are capable of yielding. By comparison, forest industry lands comprising only 14 per cent of total forest area produce 28 per cent of all wood products.

A decline in our total forest area and an enormous increase in the consumption of its products are a matter of growing concern. A 1970 appraisal of the extent and condition of our national timber resources showed that for the first time on record the forest area of the nation has declined. Over the past ten years we have lost more than eight million acres. But over the last thirty years lumber consumption has risen 49 per cent. Use of pulp products has increased 235 per cent and consumption of veneer and plywood 475 per cent. This trend is expected to continue.

Our little woodlot is hardly a molecule in the 299 million acres in private hands. But as it assumes the character of a respectable bit of working forest, capable of producing to its best within the limits of its environment, we are content that the work which gives us such satisfaction is indeed more than fun and games in the woods.

II. Timber Stand Improvement

"JUST AS AN untended garden seldom produces bumper crops of vegetables, so a neglected forest seldom produces large quantities of high-value timber. One of the major problems in forestry today is how to improve the quality of the logs that are needed to supply wood using industries. This is particularly true of the fine hardwood species."

So reads "Why TSI," the little Forest Service booklet on Timber Stand Improvement. The succinct statement is an admirable definition of our somewhat fuzzy ambitions as amateur woodlotters. Equally clear is the instruction "How We Do It":

"Weeding to remove unwanted species and make room for higher value trees.

"Thinning to relieve overcrowding and increase the growth rate of potential crop trees.

"Release of vigorous young potential crop trees for faster growth and better quality by removing overtopping trees.

"Pruning the lower stem of selected trees to produce knot free timber."

Here were our objectives, but how to make selective choices, how thin is a thinning, and how unwanted is an "unwanted species"? Where to begin on our particular hillside acres? What to do first?

WHERE TO FIND ADVICE

Our county forester, of course, held the answers. His first visit had revealed the general nature of the woodlot and what it contained. Now he proposed that we select a limited area for our first year's work. We settled on a plot of approximately ten acres on a westward-facing slope easily accessible from open pasture and a woods trail making two long sides of a triangle. Our choice of the area, in addition to its accessibility, was determined largely on the impression that it had a mixture of several varieties of growth, and what seemed, to our eyes at least, altogether too many small trees of all kinds. These appeared to be competing for space and nourishment with their taller neighbors. In many ways it was an ideal site for the beginning of our education.

And education it was. One bright morning we joined our forester at the appointed site. "I'll mark the trees to come out," he said as he loaded a pressurized paint gun with which to splash each condemned tree with a yellow spot. Wielding his squirt gun like a pistol, he traversed the area section by section while we bombarded him with questions. One kind of tree almost invariably drew a paint spot. "Why all these?" we asked. "Hop hornbeam," he said. "Around here some people call them remmen, and others lever wood. The wood is hard as iron when dry and has great bending strength. If you need a pry pole, pick a remmen sapling. It has no commercial value as a saw log, so we might as well weed it out."

Deformed young trees, three to even six inches and more at the base, all received the yellow spot. But those with straight trunks, even when growing close to one another, were usually spared. "Let them grow up a little. They are crowded, but crowding at this stage tends to reduce the number of low branches they will develop. They can be thinned out later when it will be easier to select the most promising and give them more room."

A splash on a tall maple, straight as an arrow, but only a few feet from a similar one, raised a question. "Release cutting. The big one overtops the other and shows signs of trouble. See the dead branches on one side? Better give the other one more light and growing room. Both of them can't win."

The base of our triangular plot carried many tall poplar fringing a fine grove of beech. He is going to mark all these, we thought, and then what a job we'll have. Poplar must be a weed tree, for whoever heard of a poplar board? It was just as well that we had not showed our ignorance. "Nice looking poplar there," he said. "Come spring you may want to get those to the excelsior mill. They have been offering $20 a cord. You have to peel the bark, so don't wait too far into the summer before cutting them. Do it when the sap is running."

A huge beech or old maple, its spread of branches towering over younger growth, might be given a strip of paint circling its base. "Probably too big a job for you to cut down. Girdle it if you like." This, we learned, involves making two deep cuts around the trunk, one several inches above the other. The cut must penetrate through the inner bark in order to halt the upward flow of sap. Deprived of life blood, the tree eventually dies and its bare branches no longer shade out younger growth, nor does it compete for soil nourishment. Girdling or poisoning are "quick and dirty" methods of ridding a plot of excess or weedy trees. We seldom resorted to it, however, for the dead tree is no adornment to the landscape. With no commercial goals at stake in our plans, we have preferred to leave these occasional monarchs undisturbed, to die in due time and to serve as den trees for whatever wild life might choose to take up residence.

WEEDING AND THINNING

That was a busy fall and winter of weeding and thinning. Though most of the cuttings were in small diameters, we amassed a goodly store of firewood from the larger logs we were able to reach and draw onto trail or pasture. We took time to lop off limbs and tops and spread the resulting brush over the forest floor to rot and add to the thin hillside soil. Spreading this brush proved to our own satisfaction that TSI could be done without even a suggestion of the "mess" which so many landowners seem to consider inevitable in a logging operation.

We found a ten-acre tract a bit overambitious for a more or less leisure-time avocation, and in succeeding years reduced our annual quota to five. On this reduced scale we found added pleasure in studying our woods, particularly when, after several years of

3. How a woodlot might look before, during and after a program
   of Timber Stand Improvement.

steady tutelage, our forester would O.K. our plans but tell us, "You are on your own now. See what you can do. I'll be around to check you out if you need me."

"All those decisions . . ." we complained. Ours alone to make. But we found in fact that we had developed a satisfying store of new knowledge and understanding as well as new skills of eye and hand providing endless satisfaction in shared experience and judgments. There seemed to be no fixed rules for our decisions to fell or leave standing a given tree. We learned, to be sure, of the D-plus-6 rule and occasionally applied it as a guide in some troublesome question of how far apart certain trees should be.

We found our hardwoods—predominantly maple, beech and ash—widely diversified in size and age. To apply the D-plus-6 rule required adding some forestry terminology to our vocabulary, for it applies to what is known as the *dominant crown canopy*. The *canopy* is the forest roof, the entire spread of branches overhead. *Crown* refers to the spread of branches of each tree. The *dominant* crown trees are those with the greatest spread of branches and the greatest height, and together they form the dominant crown canopy. Crowns may be large or small, depending on the accident of growing room, but the smaller crowns, if close to the height of the larger, are considered part of this canopy. These crown trees are candidates for the first harvest cutting and deserve maximum opportunity for growth.

The D-plus-6 (*diameter*-plus-6) guide applies only to the spacing of trees in the dominant crown canopy.

Tree A, in an example, has a diameter, breast high (4½ feet), of 16 inches. Adjoining tree B has a diameter of 10 inches. Adding the two diameters gives 26 inches. Divide by 2 (two trees, after all), and add to this figure (13, or D) the constant 6—and the space between these two trees should be 19 feet.

This formula is a rule of thumb some foresters disparage as a basic guide. But we have often found it encouraging when we question whether two prime trees should need what may initially appear to us to be so much growing room. To confirm its overall validity it is only necessary, for example, to measure the distance between trees in a group of fully mature and handsome maples standing by a roadside or fringing a sugar bush. If their spreading branches form the beautifully shaped crown of a freestanding tree, it is a good guess that their spacing will equal or exceed the figure produced by rule.

A more practical and perhaps more realistic basis for spacing is based on what we formed the habit of calling "Look upward, Angel." Do the leaves on one tree overhang or touch the leaves of its neighbor? Look upward and see. If this is the case one of the trees might be removed—but save the better one.

A crude example may explain the basis for this look-up idea. Consider that each leaf of a tree is the spark plug of a thousand-plus–cylinder machine. The machine is producing maximum power when every plug is firing (just like a 12-cylinder motor car). Call "power" all the elements the leaf requires to produce growth. No leaves, no growth. Leaves are blanketed —say insulated—by those of a neighbor: spark plugs (leaves) can't fire; tree is not hitting on all twelve for growth. So—one of them needs more space.

Rule and formula may be more readily applicable to a plantation forest with tree spacing predetermined by the planting. But in our own self-seeded random growth our forester's decisions were obviously made on the basis of broad experience in evaluating many elements of a particular situation. His work reminded us of a remark by a veteran builder who designed and erected a covered bridge in the town. This was a true replica of the many wooden bridges common to the past century. We had asked him what guided his choice of beam and plank to create a structure of such obvious grace and strength. Were his calculations based on technical formulas applying to this kind of construction? "No," he said, "Such things may be useful to deal with concrete and steel, but when it comes to this work, a man who can't communicate with a stick of wood better leave it alone."

Weed trees we learned to identify and eliminate because of their competition with worthwhile stock. Damaged or misshapen hardwoods that would never produce a useful saw log became more obvious as our education progressed, and these we salvaged for firewood. The relatively few maple, ash and butternut 16 to 18 inches and more in diameter were equally easy to note for a sometime harvest when we might acquire the confidence to tackle the job. But in all other—and most critical—problems in our hardwoods we continued to rely principally on the forester who was so obviously able to "communicate."

We were far more confident to undertake weeding

and thinning in areas of both red and white pine. Here there was no question about weeding out intrusive young poplar, cherry and soft maple. Most of the growth was young, with diameters from three to seven or eight inches, often growing in crowded groups with stems only a foot or two apart. This early crowding had produced tall and straight young trees, ready now for good development if given room to grow. The larger of these we pruned sparingly to five or six feet. A number of older and larger trees, overtopping the younger growth, were so irregularly shaped that even ultimate use as pulpwood was questionable. We pruned the heavy lower branches of these simply to get them out of the way and make it easier to move about for our other operations. Some we felled in order to eliminate their interference with more promising growth. A few big veterans, probably the source of the seed that had produced the smaller random growth, were left strictly alone to continue their role until a new generation could replace them.

PRUNING

The purpose of pruning is to produce clear, knot-free lumber. Knotty pine boards have some value for interior trim or panelling because of their appearance, but for all other use knots weaken a board and make lumber hard to work with and useless to turn in a lathe. A secondary and perhaps debatable virtue of pruning is the assumption that the nourishment the lopped branches no longer absorb will contribute to more rapid growth of the tree.

Pruning is seldom practiced in the hardwoods, for new branches can replace those lopped off. In the softwoods, however, no new branches will appear in the pruned area. The small scar where the branch has been cut will heal rapidly.

4. The Meylan saw has a longer reach for the higher branches.

Thinning pines we largely postponed until we had completed the initial pruning. We could then get a better view of what needed to come out, and as we removed excess trees, we often found it desirable to prune higher on the remaining trees. Then our goal was to produce clean logs up to sixteen feet, for which we would ultimately prune to seventeen feet (allowing a foot for the stump). But in no case, we had been told, should we prune to more than two thirds of the height of the tree.

Thinning the pine seemed to produce fewer problems than the hardwoods. Perhaps we had a measure of confidence from following the forester through the hardwoods and asking innumerable questions as he marked the trees we were to cut. And we were also dealing with smaller trees on the whole. Our first concern was to identify the larger diameter, good quality trees showing the greatest promise. Since they over-topped their neighbors it seemed necessary only to give them a good share of both root room and nourishment by removing some small trees nearby. These, in any case, were not likely to survive for long beneath the spread of the larger tree.

For the rest we relied largely on our "look upward" theory. We picked for survival of this first thinning the largest and most promising in the many closely packed groups, and removed the surrounding smaller trees to free them from the interference of overlapping branches. Spacing between these trees in terms of so many feet was generally ignored for the time being. A year or two of growth, perhaps more, would be time enough for a second inspection and further thinning if necessary.

Pruning, if one has the proper tools, requires little experience or skill. We have found a pruning party a means of enlisting occasional useful help and also introducing some of our land-owning neighbors to the virtues of forest care.

Meylan saw, pole saw, bow saw and short pruning saw are the tools. (These and other woods tools are discussed in some detail in Chapter 9.) The objective in pruning is to cut a branch close to the tree, leaving no stub, but at the same time making a clean cut to drop the limb without tearing bark away from the under side and without making a scar that may attract insects or disease. A stroke or two of the saw under the branch can prevent this scar.

The Meylan saw has a sixteen-inch curved blade and a three-foot handle. Blade and handle shapes combine to produce an effective cutting stroke with a minimum of effort. The metal bracket for the blade has a short hook with which to pull down a cut branch. A pole saw has a similar blade and hook on a bracket fitted over the end of a two- or two-and-a-half-inch dowel. We use a five-foot pole and another eight footer for pruning beyond the reach of the Meylan saw.

Bow saw and straight pruning saw have sixteen- or eighteen-inch blades, and are handiest on small or partly pruned trees whose branches do not interfere with reaching the trunk. The Swedish bow saw has specially shaped teeth, sharp as a razor, and is perhaps the handiest tool of the woodlotter. Blades are easily detachable, and when dull can be replaced at so little cost that resharpening is hardly worthwhile.

An axe is a poor tool for pruning. It is difficult to lop off a branch without slicing a bit of bark or even to get a clean cut close enough to the trunk to leave no projecting stub. Surrounding branches interfere with a free swing and can divert it to a dangerously glancing blow.

5. Number Two partner weeds out a damaged sapling.

We were cautioned not to thin or prune extensively along the edge of open land in order to maintain wind and weather protection for the interior trees, and to minimize too rapid a change in their environment. For the same reason it is considered poor practice to thin out so many trees within a stand that the newly admitted sun will produce undesirable weed growth.

Pruning with a chain saw is fast but forbidden by all standards of safety and good judgment. The dangers are obvious. Lopping off big branches close to the ground is hazardous enough even if the saw is started only after one is in position to make a cut, and stops it as soon as the cut is made. Moving about under limbs and over cut branches risks losing one's balance or tripping, and in the process losing control of the saw for just the instant in which the blade can do serious harm. Cutting anything more than waist high only compounds the danger and is difficult to do without creating a scar on the bark.

There are few hard and fast rules about when to prune, but the forester may point out that when the tree growth is rapid the bark is both tender and loose, and it is safer not to prune then. Winter months proved the ideal time for us. Snow depth gives an extra bit of reach. Underbrush is buried under the snow and crust and moving about is easy and fast on our skis. (Snowshoes are supposed to be the standard gear for winter woods work, but as long-time skiers we prefer the ski.) We once asked a neighbor the best time to prune apple trees. "When your knife is sharp," was the reply.

Weeding, thinning and pruning all call for a degree of subjective judgment, we found. All the rules seem to be subject to that disconcerting phrase "it all depends." How many trees should remain after a well-planned thinning? Various authorities suggest that a hardwood stand should carry perhaps 100 to 125 good crop trees per acre, destined for harvesting. Add a reasonably uncrowded "understory" of young growth to restock the stand when the crop trees have been cut. For pines and other softwoods a larger stock of 150 to 200 prime trees is possible. Much depends, of course, on variables in the quality of the site—soil, moisture, exposure. The best we amateurs could do, we decided, was to do our best without overzealous use of the chain saw. And to relish the satisfaction of striving for a relatively "clean" woodland which has at least had an assist its natural wonders to perform.

III. Felling

ADVENTURES IN CUTTING
DOWN TREES

NOTHING in the amateur woodlotter's work is more exciting than felling a big tree. The professional appears to take one look at a tree to be dropped, cranks his chain saw and knocks it over. Experience is his computer, providing automatic answers on what to do and how. Only as the amateur gains experience does he fully recognize the judgment and skill of the professional.

On many an occasion our felling of a big hardwood has called for nothing less than a full-scale family conference. This takes a little time, but we learned early on that haste is a dangerous partner in the woods. The very fact that we have given the task full consideration only adds to our satisfaction with newfound skills when everything goes well. Even much later we relish this when passing an old stump and one will remark, "Remember the time we had deciding which way to drop that one?"

First problem, of course, is the decision to drop the tree. If the forester has marked it with his splash of yellow paint, the decision has been his. But even so, we often review what he has taught us by considering his reasons for taking out this particular tree—a useful habit in guiding our own similar decisions without benefit of counsel.

34

CHOOSING THE DIRECTION OF FALL

Next comes the critical question: where can we drop it without damaging other trees as it falls? Are there promising young trees in its path which it will injure or destroy? Then if we can find room for its fall, will it cooperate by going there? Has it a heavy growth of branches that weight one side more than another? Does it lean to one side? And perhaps finally, is there a breeze that will deflect it from its appointed line at that vulnerable instant just as it starts to fall?

The slope of the ground it stands on may be a factor. Should we throw the top uphill or down? What difference, one may well ask, as long as there is plenty of room for it to fall? A good scare one day emphasized the potential hazard of felling a tree uphill. This was a big beech, a wolf tree twenty inches at the butt. There was no place to put it downhill or to one side, and its natural shape appeared to favor throwing the top uphill. All went well with the felling cut, and as the first slight widening of my cut showed that it was ready to go, we tapped the felling wedge once with a handy axe and moved aside. By good luck rather than foresight we were a good ten feet to one side of the butt when the tree crashed to the ground. The butt, rebounding on the branches pinned under the trunk as it fell, flew into the air and bounced downhill past the stump with a force that would have knocked the life out of any bystander. Thereafter we treated an uphill fall with the greatest of care, moving up hill and well away from the stump.

A downhill fall, too, needs special care, for the butt may bounce and take an unexpected flip with potentially disastrous consequences. Whatever the nature of the fall, we learned to pick a line of retreat and make it safe by clearing away brush or any other obstruction that might interfere with getting well away from a falling tree—and fast.

"Widow makers" are another hazard. These may be dead branches from the falling tree, or from adjacent trees, which break off as the tree falls. A careful survey of this danger should always take place before felling. If there appears to be the least chance of falling branches, prudence calls for getting a goodly distance away from the scene as fast as possible when the felling cut goes home.

When cutting on a hillside, the best place to drop the tree, if possible, is diagonally across the slope. Felling straight downhill on rocky or rough ground may shatter or crack the stem. Felling across a ridge or on top of a stump may also damage a good log.

THE UNDERCUT AND THE BACK CUT

First step in the felling operation is the undercut. This is a notch that removes enough wood to tip the tree off balance in the direction it is to fall. To start the undercut the saw is held at a right angle to the fall line and a horizontal cut made to a depth of a quarter or a third of the diameter of the tree. Another cut is made above this, the saw still at a right angle to the line of fall, but slicing down at an angle of

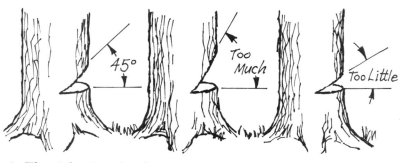

6. The right size of undercut.

45 degrees to meet the back of the horizontal cut. It may take a little practice to make this slanting cut meet the other at just the right point, but the trick is soon mastered; when all goes well, the cut away piece

7. Finishing the undercut.

will drop free or can be knocked loose with a tap of the axe.

This is the time to check the newly made notch to see that the junction of the two cuts does in fact lie at a right angle to the chosen direction. If not, additional cutting should correct the error.

The backcut starts at the opposite side of the tree from the notch, and two or three inches above the base of the notch, slicing in, again, at a right angle to the line of fall. The cut should stop about two

8. Coming in for the back cut.

inches short of the undercut. The remaining wood is
a hinge that controls the direction of the fall. A felling wedge goes in behind the saw as soon as possible,
to aid in tipping the tree in the right direction and
to prevent it from rocking back and freezing the

9. Make the back cut above the undercut and leave a hinge.

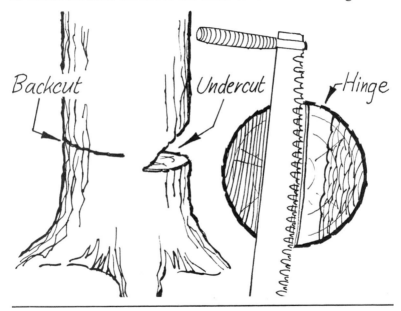

chain. The sawyer watches for the first almost im-
perceptible widening of his backcut, signaling that
the tree is off balance, held only by the hinge and
about to go. Further cutting now may destroy the
effectiveness of the hinge, but driving the wedge in
more deeply and perhaps adding another wedge for
additional pressure, will force the tree over.

A tree with a slight lean or a one-sided growth of

Problem Tree leans into others

10. Changing the direction of fall of a leaning tree by "holding a corner."

heavy branches which might pull it off the intended line can be controlled by altering the backcut to hold a corner. The side toward which the tree leans is cut away more than the opposite side. With the leaning side free and the other held by the hinge, the fall should go as planned. Additional insurance can be provided by a wedge driven into the corner of the backcut to tip the tree in the right direction.

If there is much rotten wood in the area of the felling cuts, it is safest to undercut well above the rot, even several feet higher. Because the decayed wood may not afford an adequate hinge to control direction, there is no telling which way the tree may go.

A good push at the right time is an effective way to

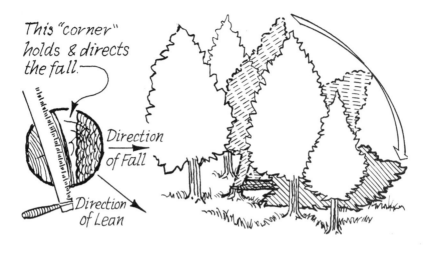

This "corner" holds & directs the fall.

Direction of Fall

Direction of Lean

force a difficult tree into the path of virtue. Handiest is a ten- or twelve-foot pole with a fork at one end— or even a point, sharpened with the axe—to get a grip on the bark. Obviously the longer the pole the better, to reach higher on the stem and thus increase the leverage; but the length will depend on what may be readily available as well as on the size and power of the helper who is to do the pushing. The sawyer must remember to get out from under as the tree moves, or the push pole may drop on him no matter how careful the helper is.

A tree leaning markedly in the direction of fall can be another problem. The weight of the overhang or lean may be such that the tree will start to fall before the backcut has reached the hinge. The trunk may

split as it falls, leaving a long, heavy splinter attached
to the stump. Cutting this involves the risk of binding
the saw, and is often better done with the axe, but in
any case the sawyer must be specially alert to get
away from this splinter as it whips free.

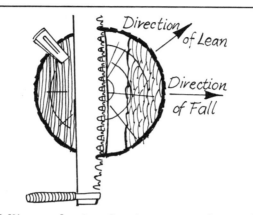

11. Use of a felling wedge in a leaning tree to change direction
     of fall.

The wind can be a help or a nuisance in felling.
A gust at the wrong time can tip a big tree back onto
the saw if there is no protecting wedge behind the
blade. A steady breeze in the right direction may
persuade a leaner to go where it belongs, but if the
wind is gusty, the sawyer needs a helper to watch the
sway of the top branches and tell him when to drive
the saw home for the final cut.

Nothing is more frustrating to the sawyer than
finding his chain saw inextricably locked into a saw
cut. Perhaps he has cut too far into the hinge and
the stem has not fallen free, but has simply tipped

over with a bit of the hinge remaining, and thus locked the chain or the blade. Or a gust rocks the tree back on the cut and nothing will get the saw out of its clutch. It is fortunate if there is another saw at hand to repeat the whole felling cut higher up the tree, above the imprisoned blade. Lacking this, the invaluable bow saw can do the same job with only a little more effort. An axe is the last resort to cut away enough wood to free the saw, but this requires great care to avoid striking any part of the blade or chain in the process.

FREEING A HUNG TREE

Next in order of frustrations is the tree that lodges in the arms of another. It can be instructive perhaps to try to decide why this has happened, but it certainly can happen occasionally to the most experienced of loggers. Simplest procedure is to hook a tractor chain on the butt and drag it away from the tree in which it hangs. Sometimes simply rocking the stem back and forth will free it from an entangling limb. Or inspection will show that if the stem can be twisted with the aid of a peavey, it will fall. If a trial with the peavey shows promise of success but more twist is needed, one can cut a pole, lash it to the peavey handle, and with this additional leverage, twist the stem free. Still another device is to put a pry block close to the butt and with a sturdy pole lever it up and back, away from the holding tree.

When none of these expedients seems practical or economical in time, there is another solution: nibble

12. Prying the butt back may free a lodged tree.

the stem away in short lengths with a series of cuts. First make a cut three or four feet from the butt. Be sure to make an undercut and if possible insert a wedge to prevent binding the saw. Then cut off another length. With each cut the shortened stem will stand at a steeper angle to the holding tree, until finally it is almost vertical and what remains can be pulled down. At worst, the top can be left hanging until wind and rot combine to let it go. The logger will at least have some firewood chunks for his pains.

When a large tree is solidly lodged in the grip of another, one last expedient remains: fell the holding tree. This is even more dangerous than the nibbling process and demands a thorough evaluation of the potential hazards. Are dead and damaged limbs ready·

to fall before the tree comes down? Can it be felled at an angle to the lodged tree? What should be done to insure that it falls the chosen way? Is there an escape route for the sawyer, free of brush or other obstruction? And is there a helper at hand who at a safe distance can call a warning as the tree starts to go?

When a really big tree goes astray and hangs up, the consequences can be abysmal. Our classic example was a towering butternut, eighteen inches at the butt, fully mature and ready for harvest and sale. It promised one Prime saw log and another either Select or Grade 1 for a premium price.

Our prize sat on a steep slope ten feet or so higher than a trail across which we planned its fall. To fell it uphill would destroy several tall maples too promising to sacrifice. A downhill course was possible, but it had to fit between another big maple and a multi-stemmed basswood below it on the edge of the trail. The gap was just wide enough but no more.

Another critical factor was its big girth, more than our lightweight saw's sixteen-inch blade would span. This meant box cutting for the backcut, the saw working in from one side of the backcut, then the other, nearly to the point of the hinge. Then the tip of the blade frees the wood between these two angled cuts. This is a slightly tricky operation but one we had managed successfully several times before.

All seemed to go well until the last move, when we neglected to recheck our progress with sufficient care and cut too deeply on the left hand side of the back cut. Thus freed, our tree started its majestic fall, not— to our horror—on line, but just far enough to the right to rest high in the arms of that blasted basswood. We derived little consolation from the thought that if we had to lodge a tree, it might as well be a good, blue-ribbon hangup.

How to get it down. . . . The butt lay just below the stump. No dragging it uphill without moving it to one side or the other of this obstacle. A long lever and 140 pounds grunting on the end made no impression. A one-inch rope through a snatch block, then to the Jeep on the trail, moved the butt clear of the stump, but directly below a projecting rock ledge. So no more business with that idea. "Cut an eight-foot saw log free, the rest of the stem will drop, and then there will be room to pull it out of that so-and-so basswood," was the next inspiration. But the steep slope below the stump put the eight-foot mark too far in the air even to scratch with the saw. As a last resort, most of the basswood had to come down before a chain and long rope to the Jeep could pull the butternut free. The salvage operation took the better part of two days before the wreckage of the basswood tops was cleaned up and the butternut bucked into logs.

"Some day," I resolved, "all my grandchildren will be gathered round my knee and I will tell them how much trouble we had getting that butternut down. And if every last one of them don't cry, I'll whup 'em good."

IV. Lopping & Bucking

HOW TO CARVE A TREE

WE HAD FELLED a tall maple with a big spread of branches—a handsome and useful tree, but badly girdled by a maple sugar borer that had signed its death warrant. Much good firewood in it, but when we cut a long log free, what a mess remained. The mass of branches stood more than head high, an obstacle to any other work in the area, and destined to be a blight on the landscape after the leaves dropped off and the bare skeleton stood high and stark in these otherwise open and graceful woods.

LOPPING

This kind of shambles is perhaps the main reason so many owners are reluctant to have any work done in their woodlands. But this ugly condition is wholly unnecessary, for a good logging contract should have a provision binding the logger to do a thorough job of *lopping*—cutting all limbs and branches so that when the log is removed nothing will be left more than knee high above the ground to show that a tree has been felled. And this debris, when strewn rather than piled, will soon disappear, first blending in with the forest floor, then rotting to enrich the quality of the soil. Hardwood brush returns to the soil in a year or two, softwood brush in a decade.

Lopping the tops and limbs thus becomes the first order of business after we fell a tree. Small branches can be cut with the lightweight axe, though a chain saw is far the faster tool. But my partner with her sharp little bow saw is almost as quick, and in our operations it is she who first clears away the small limbs while the chain saw works on anything over four or five inches in diameter.

The professional logger has a built-in dislike for this operation. To him it seems a waste of time, for he has other and more profitable work to do, and it has its elements of danger as well. One must move carefully among the tangled branches to avoid tripping or losing one's balance while the saw is running, and the saw must occasionally reach head high to cut a big limb.

A study made by the Forestry Department of the University of Massachusetts demonstrated how little time is in fact required to clean up a top. A big beech, for example, took three minutes' time for nineteen saw cuts ranging from one to three inches in diameter. Another took two and a half minutes for seventeen cuts. A bulky white pine top required thirty-one cuts and four minutes. Our amateur efforts do not match these times, but it is seldom that we need more than ten or fifteen minutes at the most to trim and spread top branches.

We timed ourselves one day when we felled a big ash for our first sale of saw logs. It was eighteen inches on the stump and had a number of massive branches. The chain saw cut two logs free, lopped off the big limbs, then trimmed these so they could be cut to short lengths for stove wood. With everything useful trimmed and ready for cutting, our time totaled just thirty minutes. When we pass the site now only a low stump is left to remind us that a tree fell there.

A hardwood top is full of useful firewood. The saying is that in slaughtering a pig the meat packers use everything but the squeal. We go just as far when felling a tree. Limbwood three inches or more in diameter is cut to short stove lengths and stacked for seasoning. Everything else is spread on the forest floor to rot.

When several trees have been felled close together or on a small area the accumulation of tops and limbs looks pretty discouraging. Cleaning up is a great deal easier if the lopping job is done on each tree right after it comes down, before felling another near it. It is then much easier—and safer—to move about freely.

If we are cutting near open land we often use limbwood and tops to make a wildlife sanctuary of sorts. A top is placed near the edge of the open ground before the branches are trimmed so that a branch or two keeps the trunk off the ground. Partly trimmed branches are thrown on top to make a good-sized pile. An opening at the base, facing the open, is the doorway through which small creatures may find haven from a soaring hawk or hungry fox.

BUCKING

After lopping, a log destined for firewood is skidded to a site chosen for a woodpile. The full, tree-length log is sometimes difficult to bring to trailside, in which case it is cut into whatever lengths are convenient to handle. A saw log is usually better left where it dropped, for bucking it to the desired length involves more problems than cutting firewood.

The first step in bucking is to get the log up off the ground to avoid sawing into the dirt. The surface under the log may seem to be only forest mulch, free from any stones. But even dirt will dull a chain, and there is no virtue in gambling that a stone may not be a few inches under the surface. Levering or rolling the log up and across another gets it off the ground and also permits the cut-off billets to drop free without binding the chain. After the first piece has been cut, a handy scheme is to lever the log up high enough to kick this piece under it and far enough back on the log to make several more cuts. Then repeat the process. If it is impractical to prop a log off the ground the only recourse is to make a series of cuts a little less than half way through the log, then roll it a half turn with the peavey and cut each piece free.

A nice refinement in bucking anything more than six or eight inches in diameter is to slant the cut slightly away from the vertical. The top of the saw blade is inclined toward the piece being cut off. Only a small angle is required to permit the cut off billet to drop free.

A *bucking wedge* of wood, plastic or aluminum is

needed when there is no practical way to keep a large-diameter log from sagging at the cut and binding the saw. (A steel wedge is no tool for the amateur logger when bucking. One touch is enough to ruin a chain.)

13. Bucking wedges prevent a big log from binding the saw.

The wedge is tapped into the cut as soon as the saw has gone in deeply enough. As the cut deepens, the wedge is tapped in more firmly. A bright-colored plastic wedge or a band of bright paint around the butt of a wood or aluminum one is a great convenience, for wedges have a habit of flying away from the log, kicked out by the chain as the cut is completed. A spot of color makes it easier to retrieve a wedge in such cases, particularly when the ground is snow covered.

How to Get the Best Value from a Saw Log

How to get the best saw logs from a tree is perhaps the most intriguing problem of the amateur. (We've dealt with it here rather than in Chapter 7 because in order to plan how best to buck up a tree, you'll need to know what the consequences of your decisions will be.) The value of a saw log is based on its quality, and quality is evaluated in terms of the log's relative freedom from defects. Standard commercial log lengths are 8, 10, 12, 14 and 16 feet. There is some flexibility as to length, and the specifications called for by the mill should always be checked in advance. Thus length, diameter and defects are the three elements that have to be evaluated to get the best possible price. A Prime log, the top grade, may bring nearly twice the price of the lowest grade. Figure 14 shows a typical list of log prices and specifications that you might receive from a mill. These specs are based on those of a veneer mill, and the prices are not current. Nonetheless, they suggest the value of the different grades, and give some idea of what mill buyers will be offering hard cash for.

Thus the first step in bucking a saw log is to measure the total salable length of the tree. This is then subdivided into log lengths that will produce the maximum price. Assume, for example, that we have a maple log that measures a total of 42 feet plus, which we want to buck up into saw logs. First we look for defects. A few here and there, but we think we can get two 16-foot logs that will grade No. 1 (First), and another one 10 feet long at the small end of the tree that will grade No. 2. Looks pretty good, for our two 16-footers will have 17- and 15-inch diameters and the 10-foot log will still give us the minimum 12-inch diameter. We'll call this break-down of our saleable length Method A (see Figure 15). Let's assume that we're going to deal with the mill whose spec sheet is shown in Figure 14. How many board feet of lumber do we have in these logs, and how much can we expect to get from the mill?

A *board foot* is defined as a square of wood one foot on a side and one inch thick. In order to deter-mine the number of board feet in a log, we need a log rule, a most ingenious device (see page 154). It's best comparable to a yardstick 30 inches long and about 1½ inches wide. One edge carries inch marks, like a yardstick but beginning 6 inches from one end, and is thus used to read diameters from 6 to 30 inches. Log lengths of 8, 10 and 11 feet are in-dicated on one face, and on the other, lengths of 12, 14 and 16 feet. Where a ruled line underlining the 12-foot length figure intersects the line marking a 12-inch diameter, for example, the figure 72 gives the number of board feet in that 12-foot log, 12 inches in diameter. This is on the so-called Vermont scale, and both sides of a section of a Vermont log rule are shown in Figure 16. Other rules, such as the com-monly used International scale, give slightly different

TO ALL LOGGERS:

New Log Specs and Prices

SPECIES	LENGTHS	PRIME	SELECT	No. 1	11" Logs	No. 2	PRICE $/M				
							P	S	#1	11"	#2
Hard Maple	6' 9' 10' 12' 13' 16'	16" & up No defects Not over 1/3 heart	14" & up No defects Not over 1/3 heart	12" & up 1 defect	11"–12" No defects 11" small dia. No sweep.	12" & up. Not over two defects	175	150	125	90	75
Yellow Birch	9' 10'	16" & up No defects	14" & up No defects	12" & up 1 defect 1½" of sweep	11"–12" No defects 11" small dia. No sweep.	12" & up. Not over two defects	205	175	135	100	85
White Birch	9'	16" & up No defects	14" & up No defects	12" & up 1 defect 1½" of sweep	11"–12" No defects 11" small dia. No sweep.	12" & up. Not over two defects	165	150	125	90	75

* All logs must have 4"–6" of trim allowance.

* Prime and select logs should be straight, have no visible defects and must be relatively round.

* Logs must be fresh cut.

* Heart of maple not over one-third of log diameter. Larger hearts will be graded as they affect the value of the log.

* Prices shown are delivered to our mill.

* This specification and Price List replaces all prior price lists.

DEFECT DESCRIPTION:

3" to 4" Sound Knot - one defect

Larger Knots - two or more defects

Slight raised curl - one defect

Burls, swells, cat faces, dote and checking, shake, curl spiral grain are defects and will be graded as they affect the value of the log.

Two or more defects in a straight line will be graded as they affect the value of the log.

Center rot or holes up to 3" in diameter well-centered and surrounded by sound wood are not considered defects; otherwise, it may be counted as one or more defects.

SCALING AND GRADING RULES:

1. Logs will be scaled with the Vermont Rule. Rule will be applied to the average of the top diameter.

2. Logs will not be cut back to increase grade.

3. No log will be accepted less than 11" in diameter—measured the average of the top.

4. Logs not meeting the within specifications will be culled.

---

14. A typical mill list of log specifications and prices (prices are not current).

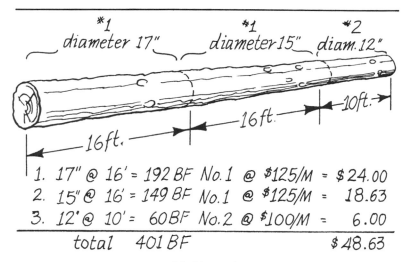

*1
diameter 17"

*1
diameter 15"

*2
diam. 12"

←— 10ft. →

←—————— 16ft. —————→|

←———— 16ft. ————→|

1. 17" @ 16' = 192 BF No.1 @ $125/M = $24.00
2. 15" @ 16' = 149 BF No.1 @ $125/M = 18.63
3. 12' @ 10' = 60 BF No.2 @ $100/M =   6.00

total   401 BF $48.63

Method A

Method B

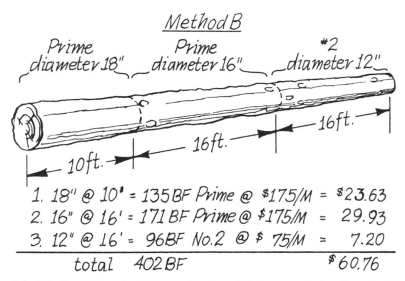

Prime
diameter 18"

Prime
diameter 16"

*2
diameter 12"

←— 16ft. →

←———— 16ft. ————→|

←—— 10ft. ——→|

1. 18" @ 10' = 135 BF Prime @ $175/M = $23.63
2. 16" @ 16' = 171 BF Prime @ $175/M = 29.93
3. 12" @ 16' = 96 BF No.2 @ $ 75/M =   7.20

total   402 BF $60.76

15. Method B bucks this saw log into higher-grade lumber (and more cash) than Method A.

volumes in board feet. Find out which rule is used in your area (from your county forester or state extension service) and go from there. The principle of the calculations is the same.

By measuring the diameter of a saw log at its small end (you can follow these calculations by referring to the drawing of the log rule), we can determine that these three logs will probably scale at the mill 401 board feet. By multiplying the board feet in a log by the price *per thousand board feet* ("$/M" in the spec sheet) offered by the mill for a given grade of timber (see the mill price list [Figure 14] and the calculations in Figure 15, Method A), we can determine that our maple logs will yield 401 board feet and $48.63. Not so bad.

But our diagram shows that a more thoughtful or expert analysis (Method B in Figure 15) would have produced almost one-quarter more money for a slight increase in volume—$60.76 for 402 board feet. Three logs of 10, 16, and 16 feet would minimize defects and upgrade two of them from No. 1 to Prime. Changing the first cut from 16 to 10 feet eliminated one defect, which went to one end of the next log. But because it was so close to the end of the log, neither it nor the other in this log were counted as defects. The largest number of defects—all that counted, in fact—were shifted to the smallest diameter log, which was obviously No. 2 grade in any case.

We once attended a forestry forum for timber growers and professional loggers staged by a mill to demonstrate good logging practice and thus, they hoped, encourage suppliers to produce better grade timber—at a resulting better price to the logger.

One demonstration consisted of felling a big maple and requiring a consensus from observers as to how best to cut it into saw logs. The tree was not altogether straight, and the question of where to cut a log to minimize this "sweep" produced many opinions but eventual agreement consistent with other obvious defects. "Cut at the point of the most abrupt crook" was the basis of the decision. The observers also generally agreed that defects should be clustered in one log as far as possible. But when a big, six-foot log was produced for examination, the fight really started, this time on what should or should not be considered a defect. Each man was an expert, in his own judgment, and the log buyer, acting as umpire, was obviously prejudiced in the mill's favor.

As we all made our decisions about which particular spots or condition on the bark qualified as defects, the log buyer marked each with a crayoned circle. When he pointed out a defect that was not particularly obvious and that had been rejected by the concensus, he marked his spot with a cross.

The log had been previously sawed into planks which were subsequently bound back into their original position by heavy steel strapping. When the straps were cut and the successive layers of the log exposed, it became evident for all to see that many of the professionals had something to learn. The obvious defects, such as knots, showed clearly on the planks, but more interesting were the debated X marks around a smallish lump on the exterior. Many of these actually represented blemishes on the interior wood that defi-

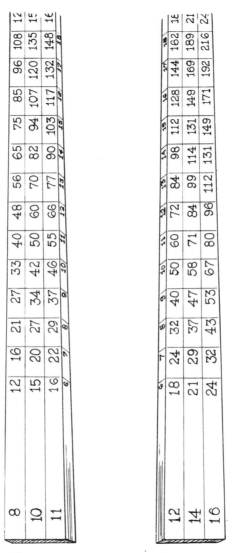

16. The two sides of a Vermont log rule. Log diameters along one edge are read against log lengths at the end to determine board feet from the body of the rule (example: 15″ diameter @ 16′ length = 149 board feet).

nitely downgraded the quality and value of a board.

"Bucking for best value" is the keynote for handling saw logs, but the amateur can hardly hope to match the X-ray eye of the log buyer in spotting defects. A few generalizations can be helpful: to minimize sweep, cut at the point of the most abrupt crook; group as many defects as possible near the end of the log; keep small surface defects grouped on the large end of the log because they may be trimmed off in the slab when the log is sawed; remember the trim allowance.

Accurate measure is of course important. A three- to six-inch trim allowance is required to permit removal of any irregularities—the butt may still have part of the "hinge" on it, or be cut on a slant, or have been shredded in skidding—at the ends of the logs. Thus it pays to make a good measuring pole. This can be a straight sapling or, better, an inch-and-a- half or two-inch dowel pole at least twelve feet long. A spike or other projection is handy at one end to hook over the end of the log. Mark off the trim allowance, and *from this point* indicate lengths from 6 feet up by two foot stages. Such a pole is handier than a flex- ible tape, for it permits one to move back and forth along a felled tree to check the best division into saw logs.

Recognizing defects, therefore, then planning how best to cut his logs, is the first task for the amateur logger who wants to turn his timber into cash. Fore- warned, he may gain some expertise by asking the right questions when cruising the woods with his forester. And of course he will learn fast when, in

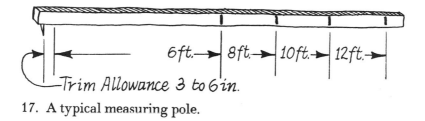

17. A typical measuring pole.

taking his logs to a mill, he is exposed to the ruthless judgments of the log buyer. Even the professionals may disagree about defects. But the learning experience provided by matching one's own wits against the mysterious messages of the defects on the outside of a log can only be heightened (when it happens) by the satisfaction of watching the mill buyer grade the log in just the same way and then receiving, for all one's hard work and occasional frustration, the mill's hard cash.

V. Skidding

HOW TO MOVE A LOG FROM HERE
TO THERE

THE HILLTOPS of our woodlot lie several hundred feet above acres of open land, and most of the hillside slopes above the woods trails vary from "strong" to "steep" and "very steep" as classified on the land-capability map prepared by the Soil Conservation Service. To bring the fruits of our labors down to trailside involved what we came to consider a full-scale course in hillside logging. With few exceptions, every tree we felled was intended to add to our harvest of firewood, or was destined for a commercial use. Everything had to come down to trailside in the log, thence to a woodpile accessible by Jeep and trailer, or all the way down to the town road for pickup by the logging truck. Logging on easier terrain would have posed fewer problems, but would not have been half the fun.

"What you two ought to have is a good crawler tractor with a winch, so you can get up these slopes or winch down your logs," the forester told us. But instead, I startled him with a demonstration of our Mighty Mouse.

Mighty Mouse (that really is its trade name) is almost too small to be called a tractor, but its crawler tracks and hydraulic bulldozer blade, and the pulling power it achieved from its one-cylinder, four-cycle motor certainly qualified it for at least a special place

18. Ready to roll a big ash log onto the log sled.

in the tractor family. For though Mighty Mouse is only three feet wide and six feet long, it seldom failed us. Unfortunately, it is probably the last of a breed made all of forty years ago, and its makers have long since turned to other products. It was ours only by happy chance. Mighty had worked for years for a good friend whose own intensive forestry program required a full-size machine. In a generous moment he offered to let me buy it, and it has been the keystone of all our operations. When Mighty gets a log to trailside, then a faithful Jeep takes over if it must be brought down over the pastures to roadside. Powerful as the little tractor is, its best pace is only six miles an hour, and the Jeep's four-wheel drive and low range gear are time savers.

We frequently used the Jeep to draw logs off the hillsides when Mighty had been left temporarily in some other part of the woodlot. If there seems to be room between trees and stumps or rocks to push the Jeep in low-low gear within chain length of a log, it is handier to make the attempt than to go get Mighty. The Jeep goes into corners where no respectable road vehicle should ever venture, and tail lights occasionally suffer when a young ash suddenly grows up right behind it as we back away with a log.

SKIDDING AIDS

A front-mounted winch would be a great asset for a Jeep. There are many occasions when a cable to reach an otherwise inaccessible log would save much time and trouble. Our make-do substitute is a good length of half-inch or larger rope and frequent use of a snatch block. Various obstructions may make it impossible to pull a log directly to the trail. The log may have to be started at an angle and moved a few feet before a clear route opens up for a straight line pull, in which case a snatch block is the only recourse. The pulley is attached to a convenient tree, from which the line can pull in the desired direction far enough to clear the obstacles. Then the log can be dragged directly to trailside. More often there is a clear passage from log to trail, but the Jeep must move along the trail at an angle to this route. A snatch block at the side of the trail is the solution.

Once at trailside, the next step is to skid the log to

a convenient assembly point for cutting to firewood lengths, or to roadside for delivery to the mill. For this we needed something to get as much of the log as possible up off the ground, both to reduce friction and to avoid an accumulation of dirt. Mills like clean logs, and may penalize for dirty ones. Dirt damages their saws, as well as the logger's, and if the log is really muddy or ice-encrusted it is difficult for the mill's log buyer to spot possible defects. Hence he is inclined to offer less for a dirty log than a clean one. We also made it a point to try to avoid tearing up the surface of the woods trails, particularly on slopes, in order to reduce the threat of erosion.

Trail skidding is no problem for the well-equipped

19. Use of a snatch block to skid out a log in close quarters.

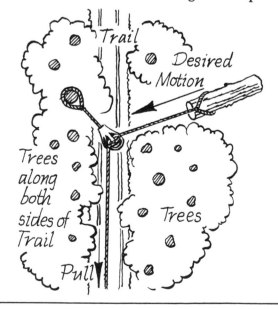

professional logger, who is likely to have a logging arch and a tractor-mounted winch. The logging arch is a wishbone-like frame on two wheels, which will carry the front end of several logs well off the ground. The three-point hitch of a farm tractor can also lift the front of the log or two and at least reduce friction with the ground.

Lacking this equipment, we improvised by making a small—and, as it proved, extremely useful—sled. We sacrificed an ancient pair of beautiful Norwegian hickory skis, made all of forty years ago—but better, we felt, to be working in our woods than gathering dust in a museum. They were 7½ feet long, but I cut them just behind the foot plate to make four-foot runners. A long-hoarded piece of four-by-four-inch oak provided two cross members to carry the log. Ten-inch blocks of this four-by-four bolted to the skis raised the cross members high enough to clear small obstructions. A heavy ring bolt was fastened through the center of the front cross member. A short length of light chain, or with small loads, a length of half-inch rope secures the logs, passing through the ring on the cross member with a couple of turns around the logs.

This little lightweight was quick and easy to make but a huskier model would be more desirable for big logs. It should have at least eight-foot runners four to six inches wide and preferably metal shod.

A so-called skid pan is often used for trail skidding. This is a flat steel pan with a rounded-up front end. Both pan and the logs it carries are chained to the tractor as closely as possible to give some lift to the front of the pan. A stone boat can be used the same way.

Where and how to acquire this skidding gear may be something of a problem, for it is no part of a hardware or building-supply store's stock. But any home carpenter who has ever built a book case or a set of shelves should be able to handle a do-it-yourself

20. The ski sled for small logs.

project as basically simple as a logging scoot. It may be necessary to buy an augur bit or two and enlist the aid of a local carpenter or builder to mill out the timber to working dimensions in his shop, and to cut the curved front end of sled runners on his band saw.

Country auctions are the best source of tools and equipment. One of these produced our favorite light-weight axe, the heavy iron nose for a stone boat, a peavey with a broken—and easily replaced—handle

and a lightweight maul handy for many uses. On
another occasion we found all the timber for a heavy
logging sled, shaped and cut to size ready for assem-
bling.

Inquiry among one's farming neighbors and a little
barn snooping is likely to produce unexpected trea-
sure. In the course of getting out some old hay for
garden mulch from a neighbor's barn, we noticed
what appeared to be an old wagon box in a corner,
half buried in the hay. Digging it out, we found that
the box was mounted on a sled with heavy six foot
runners shod with strap iron. Abandoned for years,
it was ours almost for the asking. Reinforced with a
bit of angle iron here and there, we made it serve to
bring our big logs down to roadside, though old Paul
Bunyan would have snickered at some of our expedients and a professional might well have questioned
our sanity. This sled appears in the foreground of
Figure 18.

We quickly learned the value of a peavey in rolling
a log up a ramp of short poles onto the sled. Two logs
made a load, but we occasionally could add a third
to rest on top of these. Our log lengths were 12, 14
and 16 feet, and it was tricky to balance them fore
and aft on our short six-foot rig. A chain to lash the
front end down and another at the rear needed a
chain tightener to make them snug, but this we
lacked, though it is a standard part of every log
handler's gear. It consists basically of a lever and two
hooks which, when attached to the chain, can draw
it tight with great force. Our substitute was a series

of wedge-shaped pieces of limb wood, which we drove between chain and log.

With our logs lashed down as well as we could manage, the Jeep could take our load over a logging trail to the open pasture, thence down a sidehill road of sorts to a lower field where all saw logs were assembled for trucking. But all of this was downhill and definitely on the steep side. Every trip was a contest between Jeep and sled. The Jeep had to go fast enough to keep the sled from too much yawing and pitching, but not fast enough to lose control of the whole works. Each trip down was a non-stop performance, and though the course was strewn with loose wedges and we occasionally hit the bottom with logs at a crazy angle across the sled, we always stayed right side up and never lost a log.

Only once did the best efforts of Mighty Mouse and Jeep fail to move a load of logs out for us. Several days of rain and much travel had reduced the trail surface to a slippery mix of mud and leaves. The Jeep's wheels spun and Mighty's tracks churned, but neither could draw the load up a short but steepish pitch. In desperation we hooked up a double set of pulley blocks, one to a convenient stump, and the other to the sled chain. Then the Jeep, on drier ground above the pitch, could move the load well enough, but only ten feet at a time because of the relatively short length of the rope. That way lay madness, we decided.

We admitted defeat by calling the neighbor whose big oxen had once before served our need. Their big hooves made craters in the soft trail surface as they moved our sled load, but move it they did and we were more than content to revert to this generations-old source of power.

Though a set of pulley blocks had proved impractical in this case, they saved the day on other occasions.

Pulley blocks are no part of a modern, professional logger's gear—he uses heavy log-moving machinery—but as a team of elderly amateurs, we were not ashamed to use all the help we could devise. We once rolled big, four-foot bolts of poplar to the edge of a bank from which we planned to roll them again into the trailer. They were too big and heavy to lift. But we were careless in assuming that we could bring the trailer in below them. There were no obstructions in the path we planned to take, but when we started in with Jeep and trailer we found the ground so soft that we knew we would never get out again when loaded. All those big poplar sticks would have to be lifted and moved to a trail above the stack in order to get them into the trailer. This was far beyond our strength.

A big beech limb, however, projected over the trail at just the right place for a looped rope and a double pulley block. We rigged our hoist with an ample length of half-inch rope and, with the Jeep doing the pulling, put those bolts in the trailer with the greatest of ease.

SKID TRAILS

Maneuvering logs through a woodlot requires a little care and attention to prevent damage to other trees. Stripped bark or a gouge at the base of a good crop tree encourage disease and potential loss. On side slopes, on curves or corners where a log is likely to scrape a good tree, a *bumper log* to act as a fender is a good precaution. A peavey jammed into the ground in front of a danger point and steadied by a helper is a fair one-time substitute.

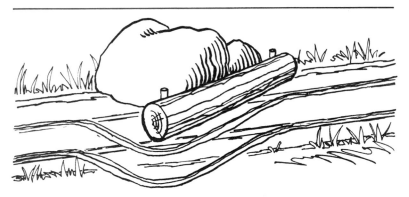

21. A fender log can help get a drawn load past an obstruction.

Designing skid trails or a road system for large scale operations is a profession in itself, but the small wood-lotter needs no such expertise. It is no great problem to cut passageways adequate for a tractor or even a Jeep by removing small trees and perhaps cutting back interfering low branches. Good crop trees, of course, should be spared, and steep grades and marshy ground are obviously to be avoided. On any slope, however, there should be water bars to prevent gullying or erosion. Stumps should be cut close to the ground, particularly the stubs of small saplings which are a hazard to a soft tractor tire and nasty for the unwary foot. Cutting close to the ground is hard on a chain saw, but if dirt and leaves are kicked away, a sharp bow saw will do the job.

VI. Firewood

HOW TO FILL THE WOODSHED

FEW OCCUPATIONS can give the woodlotter more satisfaction than cutting his own firewood. One may wonder whether this does not in part stem from deep-rooted instinct dating back to primitive man, for whom fire was both a mystery vouchsafed by his gods and a necessity for his existence. However one might speculate, to wield saw and axe with one's own hands and for one's own purposes is a refreshing escape from the impersonal technology of modern living.

Gathering firewood may well be the first purposeful introduction to a woodlot. For many a city-bred owner firewood is likely to be the first reason for recognizing his wooded acres as something more than scenery. From this gentle spark of interest may come the impulse to do something constructive with the land.

This is to assume, however, that it carries at least some proportion of hardwoods, for only these species provide a log fit to put in the woodshed. Pine, spruce and other so-called softwoods will of course make a fire, and they supply stove wood in areas lacking hardwood growth, but the woodlotter in hardwood country will ignore them except perhaps to supply kindling.

The gases generated by combustion of these resinous woods, even when burned in a hot fire, produce an accumulation of creosote that is the source of most chimney fires. In old chimneys, which may lack a ceramic tile lining, creosote can soak through the brick and spread to adjacent wood in a black stain that is impossible to clean or cover. A tiled chimney may prevent this stain but can still accumulate enough creosote to produce a frightening and potentially destructive fire.

HEAT VALUES: DRY *vs* WET WOOD

The best fuel wood has relatively high density, (weight for volume), burns steadily but not too rapidly, and makes a "clean" fire when seasoned long enough to be called dry. *Dry* is, of course, a relative term. Only a kiln or oven will reduce moisture content to near zero, whatever the wood. Research has shown that good "dry" hard maple—one of the best of woods—will retain on the order of 25% moisture after a year's open air seasoning.

Dry wood is the key to a good fire. Partially dry wood will burn after a fashion but as its moisture boils off up the chimney the condensation will produce creosote. Hence wood that is not properly dry should be burned in a hot fire to minimize this problem. Any smoldering fire of steaming damp wood is likely to produce little heat and much possible trouble.

Ash is one happy exception to this rule, because it will burn before it is really dry. For this reason it is our choice for small kindling. Since the production of kindling wood is usually the last stage in our cycle of firewood operations, a few days of open air drying in late summer or fall conditions a winter's supply—split fine to approximately two inch sticks—well enough to stack in the woodshed for immediate use.

Heat value drops dramatically with increased moisture content, as one might expect. If we assume dry wood seasoned outdoors for 12 months has a relative heat value of 100% at a moisture content of 25 per cent of oven-dried weight, green wood cut in fall, winter or spring may have a moisture content of 78 per cent and a heat value of only 65 per cent. The relative heat value, air dry and green, is suggested by Table 1.

Table 2 may be particularly useful in deciding when to fell cull trees for firewood, and reveals also the importance of proper seasoning in increasing fuel value, and the usefulness of "leaf felling" to promote drying. In this case branches and leaves are left on the tree for two weeks or more. Moisture lost through the leaves accelerates the drying process. Data for these tables and this discussion are drawn from the instructive pamphlet "Firewood for Heat," prepared by a research forester, Peter H. Allen, and published by the Society for the Protection of New Hampshire Forests in Concord, N.H.

Our own firewood cutting takes no account of the seasons. Our first enthusiastic response to the pleasure of producing our own wood yielded more than a winter's supply. Hence we were able to adopt a cycle that left a year's stock to season in its original stacks for the following year. Thus everything that comes into the woodshed has had twelve to fifteen months to dry in the open.

TABLE 1: APPROXIMATE FUEL VALUES FOR 20 TREES

Species	Available Heat Units (Million BTU/90 cu. ft. wood)*		Weight (lb. per cu. ft.)	
	Air Dry	Green	Air Dry†	Green
BEST				
Locust, Black	26.5	24.4	48	58
Hickory, Shagbark	25.4	23.8	51	63
Hop hornbeam (Hornbeam)	24.7	23.5	—	—
White Oak	23.9	20.4	47	63
Maple, Sugar	21.8	19.6	44	56
Birch, Yellow	21.3	19.4	44	57
Ash, White	20.0	18.0	41	48
MODERATELY GOOD				
Maple, Red	19.1	17.6	38	50
Cherry, Black	18.5	17.3	35	45
Birch, White or Paper	18.2	16.7	38	50
Maple, Silver	17.9	16.4	33	45
Elm, White	17.7	15.8	35	54
POOR				
Tamarack	19.1	18.1	37	47
Pine, Pitch	18.5	16.4	—	—
Pine, Norway	17.8	16.8	34	42
Hemlock	15.0	12.8	28	50
Red Spruce	15.0	14.2	28	34
Butternut	14.3	12.2	27	46
Basswood	12.6	11.0	26	42

(BTU—the quantity of heat required to raise the temperature of one pound of water by one degree Fahrenheit. Abbreviated British Thermal Unit.)

TABLE 2: HARDWOOD SEASONING, MOISTURE CONTENT, AND FUEL VALUE

Condition of Wood	Moisture Content (% of oven-dried weight)	Relative Heat Value (% of value for air dry)
Green in fall, *winter, or spring*	78	65
Green in summer	64	—
Two weeks after *leaf-felling in summer*	45	—
Spring wood *seasoned 3 months*	35	85
Spring wood *seasoned 6 months*	30	93
Dry wood *seasoned 12 months*	25	100

SOURCE: Peter H. Allen, "Firewood for Heat," Bulletin 17, Division of Resources Development, N.H. Department of Resources and Economic Development (Concord, N.H.: Society for the Protection of New Hampshire Forests [1974]).

* A legal cord contains a net wood volume of approximately 90 cubic feet.
† *Air dry* wood no longer experiences a net moisture loss to the surrounding air, and contains about 25 per cent moisture in outdoor storage.

SOURCE: Peter H. Allen, "Firewood for Heat," Bulletin 17, Division of Resources Development, N. H. Department of Resources and Economic Development (Concord, N.H.: Society for the Protection of New Hampshire Forests [1974]).

The specter of an energy crisis lends interest to the value of a cord of dry firewood from one's own woodland. A little arithmetic gives a clue. Dry sugar maple, according to our table, yields 21.8 million BTU for 90 cubic feet or one cord. (This is based on the accepted assumption that a 128-cubic-foot legal cord —4 foot lengths stacked 4 feet high in a pile 8 feet long—as stacked contains an actual net volume of approximately 90 cubic feet of wood.) At $40 a cord one million BTU has a value of $1.83. The same heat value—one million BTU—of home heating oil (which yields 140,000 BTU per gallon) at 30¢ per gallon carries a price of $2.14. To cope with variable costs of cordwood and oil, one can assume that the cost of dry hardwood roughly equals that of fuel oil when wood costs one and a half times as much in dollars per cord as oil costs in cents per gallon. Put in other terms, one can estimate that a cord of dry hard maple has a heat value of approximately 156 gallons of oil.

Thus a program of firewood cutting serves a dual purpose for the thrifty woodlot owner, reducing his oil bill and materially improving the character and future productivity of his land.

Firewood, however, is not always the best end use for a weed tree or condemned hardwood. Locust, while dense and thus desirable for the fireplace or stove, makes the best of fence posts and might better be saved or sold for this purpose. Locust posts have been found that have been in the ground for some thirty years without deteriorating. Butternut, too, though classed as moderately good for firewood, is first choice of many farmers for fence posts, sharing that rank with ash. Their logs split easily in fence-post lengths.

Ash has a ready market in logs of at least 10 inches in diameter and other hardwoods in diameters from 12 inches or larger are acceptable saw logs, occasionally in lengths as short as six and eight feet.

As a general rule, it is well to examine carefully any hardwood fourteen to sixteen inches or more DBH that has been marked for cutting in a Timber Stand Improvement program. If the potential log is relatively free from defects it may be better to avoid felling it until a harvest cutting can be made, when it can be sold with the rest of the crop. Trees of this size may be condemned because of injury or disease that prevent further growth, or so weaken the stem that it is likely to fall under the stress of wind and weather, possibly damaging adjacent trees of good quality.

Ash is perhaps the easiest to split, though maple, beech and butternut run a close second. This easy splitting, of course, makes ash the prime choice for kindling. Elm is notoriously tough, and no apologies are necessary to discard a chunk whose resistance is amplified by big knots. Hornbeam is almost as tough as elm. Apple and cherry burn well, and apple will produce flame color that adds to the charm of an open fire—but they can be pure horror to split.

There is one exception—and there may be more beyond our experience—to the dry wood rule I men-

tioned earlier and that is dead sumac. On many an
abandoned pasture and often in a random growth of
pine, sumac will thrive on the poorest soil imaginable. Some of the largest stems may be four inches
or more at the base and the many crooked branches
may rise fifteen feet or more. The tree has a not un-
attractive reddish brown "blossom," delectable for
certain birds. But it is nevertheless a weed, and from
the point of view of the woodlotter, it was created
only to be cleared out of his woods and pastures, and
perhaps more importantly, to supply the most useful
kindling material imaginable.

Devotees of the Cape Cod or soapstone firelighter
or of a squirt of kerosene with which to start a blaze
in fireplace or stove need not apply for sumac kindling. But those who find the lighter or kerosene system objectionable from the point of view of smell and
bother may well keep an eye open and collect dead
sumac. The "dry" specification notwithstanding, a
piece of sumac can be plucked out of the ground in
a wet pasture, split open with a jackknife blade, and
thin shavings stacked tepee-wise to form the base of
an open air picnic fire. No one passes our picnic fire
test until this sumac trick and a single match suffice
to produce a proper campfire. Even half-dry sumac
twigs with a few larger diameter sticks on top will
give stove or fireplace blaze a running start.

Somewhere in these pages we have maintained
that we use every bit of a felled tree but the leaves
and twigs—anything, in fact, over three inches in diameter. Bits and pieces, perhaps, but nevertheless useful when a quick blaze in the little stove comfortably

takes the chill out of a sharp morning, and the fire
need last only an hour or so.

SPLITTING TOOLS AND THEIR USES

Splitting firewood is best done with splitting hammer and steel splitting wedge. The axe may well
handle anything under six or eight inches diameter.
A razor sharp axe is considered a dangerous tool for
splitting. Best choice is one with a relatively heavy
head and long handle, with an edge filed to a broad
V, the better to blast open a crack than bury itself in
the wood by penetrating too deeply. A sharp thin
blade, penetrating rather than splitting, tends to
"freeze" in the wood.

Efficiency calls for a solid base on which to stand
the billet—a short chunk of hardwood or the flat
top of a stump. The forest floor or anything but very
hard-packed ground will act as a shock absorber for
some of the energy one puts into the swing of the
axe, and will decrease the effective force of the blow.

One can save energy, too, by resisting the impulse
to separate from the chunk by hand pieces still held
on by strips or slivers. Reach for the lightweight
axe—with a thin edge well sharpened—and slice
through these slivers to free the two parts.

Experience soon teaches the tricks of the trade: the
full swing of the splitting hammer, the ability to hit
the same spot two or three times in a row when
necessary, the recognition of crooked grain or a bad
knot which may involve splitting off a slab before
striking dead center on the billet.

The best time to split wood? One school of thought maintains that green wood, fresh cut, splits more easily than dry. Another believes frozen wood is the easiest. Our experience tends to verify the fresh wood notion, but it is questionable whether there is laboratory-tested evidence to prove a case. As one old timer said, "I reckon you can split wood most any time you got the gumption. Hit it hard enough and it'll split."

How long does it take to split a cord? Quite a while, is the best answer in our experience. Ten years of woodlotting and another ten, maybe, of occasional chances to swing a maul have left no statistical records of our own performance. But any one who thinks to earn a living in the firewood business had better acquire or lease a mechanical splitter. These machines, increasingly evident in recent years, force a fireplace log against a cleaver by a hydraulic ram. One operator whose year around business is firewood declares that this machine helps produce a cord of wood, split and stacked, in three man hours.

BUCKING AND STACKING

Felling a tree, then cutting it to fireplace lengths, is the least time-consuming of operations in fuelwood production. To check this to our own satisfaction, we one day picked a fifty-foot-tall maple for a test case. Felling took five minutes—longer than usual because we spent a minute or two debating the direction to fell it because of two nearby trees. Once the tree was down, we started ten feet from the top, where the stem was perhaps three inches in diameter, and moved down toward the butt, using the chain saw to cut sixteen-inch pieces. In ten minutes this job was completed and we had thirty pieces of stove wood ready to toss to a nearby stacking site. A minute or two less might have been the time had the stem been up off the ground for its full length, but in two sections it was necessary to make cuts half through, then roll these sections half a turn and complete the cut.

One effective way to speed firewood production when working with small diameter trees—up to five or six inches in diameter—or with small limbwood is to do a gang cut. The small logs are assembled side by side and others laid on top, all supported off the ground by small logs or billets lying at right angles to the stack at frequent intervals. A single pass of the chain saw thus cuts a number of pieces at a time. Arranging the logs in position and even using a chain around the pile to hold it all together takes a little time but makes for a high production rate compared to cutting single logs.

If a considerable quantity of limbwood or other small-diameter stock has been assembled, it may pay to build a more ambitious rack to hold the wood in place for a gang cut. Drive rows of posts to form a frame a foot and a half or two feet apart. Space the posts in line at eighteen-inch intervals if cutting to that length, or space them to whatever length may be desired. Make the frame long enough to accommodate the average length of the pieces to be cut up. Then put small logs crosswise along the bottom of the frame to keep the logs off the ground and avoid running the saw chain into the dirt. The stock to be cut can then be stacked in the rack for successive gang cuts close to each post.

For one-time use in the woods, building such a rack takes rather too much time to be profitable, but if small-diameter firewood stock is to be all brought to a central point the rack has obvious advantages.

When making up firewood we try to assemble as many logs as practical at a trailside spot easily accessible for the Jeep and trailer. Close by should be a pair, or even better, three trees to bracket the woodpile. As a foundation for the stack, two or three sturdy saplings or small logs are placed side by side lengthwise between the trees. These are supported by short logs laid crosswise, so that the bottom tier of firewood chunks is well off the ground. Care must be taken to make this foundation structure level, so that a shoulder-high stack will not topple over in the course of a year or more of seasoning. The foundation stringers can be laid on a slope if the bracketing tree on the downhill side is husky enough to hold the stack.

Freestanding stacks can, of course, be made anywhere—prop trees not being available—by cribbing the ends of the stack, or by holding the stack ends with sapling poles at each end. These are anchored by first pushing the butts into the ground a few inches, then joining them with wires running the length of the stack after it has been built up two or three feet. Another set of wires can be added at a higher level.

The standard four-foot length of a pulpwood stick makes possible a handy stack used by some professionals. A pair of stakes are driven into the ground eight feet apart. When the wood is stacked, the stakes are connected with eight-foot saplings notched at each end. The notches fit over the stakes and hold the pile together—a neat and accurate measure of one cord.

Having a third tree handy for another stack is a convenience when bucking for both fireplace wood and shorter pieces for the stoves. Each size then has its own stack.

Trailside seasoning as opposed to woodshed drying calls for some degree of protection for the open-air stacks. Handiest for this are sheets of corrugated metal roofing, salvaged wherever and whenever opportunity offers. These are usually eight feet long by thirty inches wide, though longer sheets are obtain-

22. Part of next winter's stove wood stacked for seasoning.

able. These overlap the sides of the stack and make
good protection from rain or snow and they are practically everlasting for this use. Equally effective, but
good only for a season or two, is the black tarred paper
used for roofing and siding. A roll of this material
will supply stack cover for several years. The cost of
a roll is less than a single sheet of corrugated metal.
After covering the stack, scrap chunks and logs must
be laid across the top to hold the covering in place.

When relatively small amounts of firewood can
be produced, bucking and stacking firewood at the
felling site is a practice we soon learned to avoid.
Small accumulations from only one or two trees are
usually buried under winter snows, thus losing good
possible drying time in the open air, and they have
also a surprising way of getting "lost." It is only
natural to want to get the big stacks into the woodshed first. After these have been transported, there
just doesn't seem to be room for the little collections
scattered about, and they may be overlooked for so
long as to be of little value when collected.

The specific qualities of various tree species in
terms of BTU content and density add interest to the
choice of firewood, but the poet makes a graceful and
perhaps more memorable statement in the following
lines:

IN PRAISE OF ASH

Beechwood fires are bright and clear
If the logs are kept a year.
Chestnut only good, they say,
If for long 'tis laid away.
But ash new or ash old
Is fit for queen with crown of gold.

Birch and fir logs burn too fast.
Blaze up bright and do not last.
It is by the Irish said
Hawthorn bakes the sweetest bread.
Elm wood burns like churchyard mold,
E'en the very flames are cold.
But ash green or ash brown
Is fit for queen with golden crown.

Poplar gives a bitter smoke,
Fills your eyes and makes you choke.
Apple wood will scent your room
With an incense like perfume.
Oaken logs if dry and old,
Keep away the winter's cold
But ash wet or ash dry
A king shall warm his slippers by.

VII. Cash from the Woodlot

IN THE INNOCENT pleasure we found in working in the woodlot there was little consideration of whether we could actually sell anything from it. To be sure, many trees were large enough, even to our initially inexperienced eyes, to make a commercial log. To bring in a logger and his machinery and subject the lot to a commercial logging job was farthest from our minds.

But as we gained knowledge and experience over the first two years of our gradual progress in weeding and thinning, it became obvious that we might, in fact, produce something salable on a do-it-yourself basis.

For a larger woodlot than our 80-some acres a careful survey of its resources would perhaps have been desirable. But in the course of our forester's general survey of the area and his several visits to mark trees for weeding and thinning, we had acquired an intimate knowledge of what it contained and had learned something of the relative values of the several species. Had we contemplated even on our own small scale selling all the marketable ash and maple, for example, it would have been appropriate to ask a forester to cruise the lot for a detailed estimate of what was available. Bids would then be solicited from loggers, and the sale made under contract.

A logging contract sets a fixed price per thousand board feet for each species. Terms of payment are set, and the logger agrees to submit, in verification of the amount due the seller, records from the mill showing the number of board feet he delivers. Equally important to the owner are provisions governing the character of the logger's work. To what extent will he reduce slash, for example, by cutting all tops and limbwood so that nothing above an agreed height will be left standing to affect the appearance of the forest? What are provisos for logging roads, if any? How long a period will the work cover? Will the logger give a performance bond to insure his compliance with all terms of the contract? These and other items are so critical that one's first logging contract should be made in consultation with a forester.

Our forester's advice guided us to our first sale. "You have quite a lot of good-sized poplar," he pointed out one day. "There is a steady market for this at a mill making excelsior. If you can hire a truck to get it over there, maybe 20 miles, you can turn it into cash."

A phone call to the mill brought assurance that they would be glad to have any quantity, however small, at a base price of $20 a cord plus a varying transportation allowance of a dollar or two. Next day's mail brought a specification sheet calling for peeled bolts of 4-inch-minimum diameter, and 49-inch length, small crooks acceptable.

We learned that poplar can be readily peeled in

the early spring, as soon as the sap starts running,
and that the peeling is accomplished by slicing a
groove through the bark the full length of the tree
with the tip of a chain saw, then prying the bark
away with a spud. This is a small lever, a metal bar
six to perhaps ten inches long and one and one-half
to two inches wide, sharpened to a dull chisel point
at one end and preferably slightly curved. From a
borrowed example we made two of our own from an
automobile spring leaf.

For several years harvesting poplar was the first
order of business in April and early May. Practice
developed a team operation that produced a peeled
log at an average net time of about thirty minutes.
Two cuts for the undercut, another for the felling
cut, usually aided by a wedge if the tree was large
enough, and the tree is down. The chain-saw man
then walks the length of the tree, the tip of his saw
cutting a groove through the bark well into the white
wood. At the same time, the distaff member of the
team starts to loosen the bark, working at the butt
end and inserting the point of the spud under the
bark to pry it loose from one side of the log. After
cutting the peeling groove, the saw moves back toward the butt lopping all limbs close to the trunk.
The saw is then exchanged for another spud. Starting
again at the butt, the partners work together on
opposite sides to free the bark the full length of
the log.

Nothing in the world is more slippery than this
peeled log and its bark. Even on gentle slopes a nudge
with the peavey was enough to start the log tobog-

ganing downhill to a collecting point from which it was moved to a yarding center for cutting into bolts.

Over the next several years we doubled and tripled our initial two-cord harvest before consuming most of the available stock. But poplar has a comparatively rapid growth, and the smaller trees we left standing will insure another harvest in a few years.

This does not suggest that we had adopted a sustained-yield concept for the poplar. Poplar has the least value of the several species in the woodlot and hence receives no favors if it interferes with the growth of better-quality trees.

It is a commentary on the effect of changing times on wood utilization that the excelsior mill was finally forced to close for lack of raw material. Farmers in the region whose woodlots had been the principal source of supply would not deliver their poplar at the prices offered, and economics evidently forbade any appreciable increase in what the mill could pay. Other woodlot owners, many of them non-residents, neglected to take the opportunity to improve the quality of their land by clearing out these short-lived trees whose sale would cover the cost of the required labor.

Ash, maple and beech appeared to be our most plentiful trees, but we made no attempt for several years to take more than a casual inventory of this growing stock. But when last logged over, some thirty years ago, many that were not yet large enough to harvest profitably had been left to continue their growth and to restock the woodlot. Some had now reached a healthy maturity, and these we noted as candidates for a sale of selected saw logs. As we gained experience and confidence, we determined to get them out ourselves.

We learned that a ready market existed for ash over ten inches in diameter for split-rail fencing and implement handles. But we were after larger game, and if we found we had enough larger trees to make a truckload, we would harvest only the largest and allow the younger stock more years to develop. A forester suggested that a plywood mill offered better prices for high-grade logs, and would accept butternut as well as ash and maple.

But we had also been told that we should make reasonably sure a mill would accept a load of logs when offered. We had heard of instances when a mill, perhaps overstocked with logs or lacking demand for the category offered, would accept a truck load only at a considerable discount from the anticipated price. A call to the mill produced a copy of their specifications and price list and assurance that they would be in the market for our logs. The mill also put us in touch with a trucker who agreed to pick up our logs and deliver them to the mill.

The next step was a more careful survey of the trees we had identified as eligible for harvest, so that we would cut no more than the approximately 3000 board feet the trucker said would make a load. We lacked the calipers foresters use to determine tree diameters, but had found a table that translated circumference to diameter (This is reproduced in the back of this book at the end of the Glossary of Terms and Units of Measure). Finding the circumference, measured breast high (4½ feet) on the trunk, we consulted our table to find the corresponding diameter. Our log rule would then give us the number of board feet in the log. But here we had a problem. How long was the log to be? Some of these big trees would undoubtedly give us two logs, some might have only one good twelve footer, or even a sixteen footer. It was obvious that we might run up a big error if we tried to compute our desired 3000 feet from the measure of standing trees. The professionals know how, but we had not taken that forestry course in school. Our solution was the obvious one: fell our largest trees first, cut the one or two logs they provided, measure these, then see what we had accumulated. With the help of a log rule (Vermont scale), some lucky guesswork, and the methods described in Chapter 1 in the section called "How to Get the Best Value from a Saw Log" our amateur efforts were rewarded when the trucker picked up our assembled logs and said "Enough—must have a good 3000 feet there now." Only four small logs remained on the ground, none of them of much value.

Happy ending to our first adventure in full-scale logging was the check from the mill for $416.69. This was certainly more than the ten cents an hour we estimated as our wage for other operations. Though far from subsistence income, it nevertheless proved that an occasional sale of quality logs plus the smaller but more frequent payments for poplar and the small annual amounts from the Agricultural Conservation Program definitely covered out-of-pocket expenses for all our work.

(The Agricultural Conservation Program was established by the federal Department of Agriculture to encourage, among other things, planned conservation practices by forest and woodlot owners. Administered by a county agency and supervised by a county forester, it provides federal payment of 70 per cent of the cost of woodland improvement not to exceed $25 per acre, as well as 50 per cent of the cost of erosion control measures on logging roads. The original ACP was renamed REAP—Rural Environmental Agricultural Program—and again more recently RECP for Rural Environmental Conservation Program.)

There was special satisfaction from our mill check, for the log buyer's tally sheet showed a high percentage of Select and First grade logs—testimony to the success of our effort to identify and fell only trees that would produce a good return. Prime ash, for example, brought us $175.00 per thousand, Select $150.00, and First grade $135.00. Ninety per cent of the ash was in these grades. The same percentage applied to the butternut at $150.00 per M for Select and $135.00 for First. Less than 300 board feet was graded at $90.00.

The difference in value between grades as determined by the log buyer at the mill lent tangible evidence to the professional foresters' objective: to grow good quality trees as well as more and larger trees by adhering to good management practices.

Firewood is, of course, the most obvious saleable product of a woodlot. It is always in demand and brings steadily increasing prices. But our program of thinning and culling produced no more than an ample supply for our own use because of the limited size of each year's planned project. It was enough to have a full woodshed and somewhat more than the next year's supply stacked and seasoning in the wood-lot.

Many an owner of substantial woodlot acreage, however, has found firewood income a means to reduce the net cost of an extensive one-time improvement program. Trees to be felled are marked by the forester, and the owner can make a contract with a logger on the basis of an agreed price per cord. Or a consulting forester (whose expertise is essential for this type of sale) will cruise the area and estimate the number of board feet of timber available. Then the logger pays by this measure.

There are other woodlot by-products, not neces-sarily providing much cash, but always gratifying. Limbwood, crooks, short billets from a saw-log end and the low-graded discards from a crop tree are the raw material for an infinite variety of objects to be tinkered up at the home workbench.

We had set aside a straight piece of butternut some five inches in diameter one day, after felling and bucking out a saw log. It was destined for a fence post. In an idle gesture we peeled the bark from one end and found a beautiful pattern of dark and light brown wood beneath. That post came home with us, and after a few months' seasoning, a sixteen-inch length made a handsome base for a tall table lamp. Half-inch slices consumed the rest. Sanded and polished, these made attractive coasters and welcome small gifts at Christmas time. Collecting bits and pieces ten or more inches in diameter eventually produced, in the same way, useful and equally attractive small, round cutting boards. The same things can easily be done with well-dried rock maple.

One big butternut saw log developed a check or split at one end and produced a three-foot billet when this defect was removed. We used the chain saw to slice this lengthwise into thick slabs. These are seasoning until the day we find time to cut them on a table saw into inch or inch-and-a-half strips, run these through a planer to get uniform pieces an inch thick and glue them together with alternating strips of light and dark wood. The product will be another attractive cutting board.

VIII. To Plant a Tree

To THE AIR traveler flying over most of the eastern states the land below appears to be one huge forest. The carpet of greenery is spotted with farm land, most prominent in the soil-rich valleys, but the over-all impression is trees, trees and more trees. Vermont is 74 per cent forested, Maine has even more, and the entire area is two-thirds to three-quarters covered by trees.

These green acres arouse mixed feelings in the forester and the conservationist. The former sees an enormous economic asset whose productive output is probably only a half to two-thirds of its potential for lack of even the most elementary management. The latter may be content with the vastly important contribution this greenery makes to climate, soil, and water, but he may also be concerned with the grow-ing threat of destruction imposed by the forces of industrial and urban expansion. But both can take some satisfaction in the new and growing attention to problems of land use and pollution.

The forester, however, sees more than acres of un-productive woodlands. Fields and hillsides that once were crop land or pasture now lie deserted and ne-glected, growing scrub pine, clumps of juniper and weeds. Once an adequate economic base for a small farm, their former resources have become too limited for profitable farm operation. New economic and social forces have taken the farmer and his sons off to other occupations, and the land has passed to nonresident owners.

Here, then, are acres that play no useful part in the economy. Planted to pine or other species appropriate to their site, they can return a substantial economic increment and play a part as well in contributing the manifold additional benefits of forest cover. These are more substantial than is commonly appreciated. It is said that the forest acts like a great buffer to ameliorate the extremes of wind, sun and rain. It can reduce wind velocity by 20 to 60 per cent and intercept rain and snow to reduce annual precipitation reaching the ground by 15 to 30 per cent. As a natural air conditioner it can reduce maximum summer air temperatures by 10 per cent, and absorb and reflect some 90 per cent of visible radiation.

"But . . ." says the environmentalist who sees beyond the trees to the whole panorama of hill and valley, forest and field. "But what of the landscape? There is more than one kind of desert. Are we to have no relief from the solid mass of the forests? Field and forest make the pattern we so admire. Let us keep some open space."

And here lies a dilemma. Shall the woodlotter fill his open land with a plantation, or is the quality of his landscape such that the choice is to leave it unchanged? Planting and even minimal management will produce a financial return. Open land will require annual care. Onetime cropland can perhaps be restored to hay or pasture. Whether either of these latter uses is economically viable depends on factors only the owner can evaluate, and many of these may be unpredictable. At any rate, the land will always be there.

WHERE AND WHAT TO PLANT

A forecast is somewhat simpler to prepare for a plantation. First step is to determine the quality of the site. Here again the forester and the Soil Conservation Service are the authority on which to rely for this major determination. Soil and topography will determine the area and to some extent the choice of what to plant. How much of the area is to be planted remains the owner's choice. Accessibility is a factor also to be considered, for there will be work to do for man and machine. Several small areas may be selected for planting rather than one large plot. The quality of the landscape as well as topography come into play in this respect. Five-year-old pines are a carpet on hill and field, but fifteen years later their wall will be a curtain—a new horizon. Will these mature trees destroy a cherished view? It may be wise to plan ahead.

What to plant is the next question. It is sometimes possible to make a good guess about what will grow on the site by observing what is growing on similar sites. What trees border the open land? Are there any obvious factors that would preclude their growing in the plantation? One, certainly, is the exposure to which new seedlings will be subjected. Many species require early protection from the sun, while others are more tolerant.

Here again the forester must be the guide. He will

not only match species to the soil, but from his experience with other plantations in his region will have well-tested advice, not only on species, but on all other aspects of cultivation and management of this new enterprise.

More likely than not he will recommend red or white pine, for pine is the pioneer of the eastern forest and is adaptable to a variety of sites and soils. Red pine does not need the shade of other growth, will grow on dry soil, and is less subject to disease than the white pine. White pine wants more moisture—but not wet soil—will tolerate shade, but is subject to blister rust and the white pine weevil. These hazards need watchfulness and can be mitigated by prompt attention and treatment. Both are long-lived trees, and both will produce posts, pulp cuttings, and saw logs at about the same time span. Soil, exposure, and the degree to which intensive cultivation can be practiced determine the growth rate and the periods for intermediate harvests before they reach sawlog size some 25 years after planting.

One Vermont red pine plantation, under the most intensive cultivation, has produced something salable annually from its fifteenth year to its sixtieth. A municipal forest, reported by the state forestry deparment, produced revenue of $51.00 per acre for thinnings alone over a thirty-five–year period after planting, and at that time its standing timber had a value of over $180 per acre.

Red and white pine are not, of course, the only species open to the plantation planner. Scotch pine, balsam, larch, and spruce are among other choices.

The forester is best qualified to point out their relative merits. The hardwoods, including maple and ash, are not likely to be included on his list. Hardwoods can be planted under the right conditions, but such plantations are not common. Reproduction of maple and ash either by planting or natural seeding is practically impossible in some areas where in recent years the deer herd has far exceeded the natural food supply and destroys these for forage. Scotch pines are subject to severe damage by the porcupine in northern areas, to such an extent that state forest authorities combat the problem by releasing a fisher cat in damaged areas to reduce the porky population.

PLANTATION LAYOUT

How many trees to plant will be determined by the area selected and, more significantly, by the spacing between the seedlings and between the rows. For a purely ornamental planting, such as a single group of a few trees or a row of a dozen or so, minimum space between seedlings should be six feet for white and eight feet for red pine. More space will encourage a fatter growth if screening is the objective. But for a plantation, six-, seven-, or eight-foot spacings are most often chosen. Twelve-foot spacing has on occasion produced unusually rapid growth, but this figure does not seem to be generally acceptable.

Decision on how far apart to plant seedlings and space the rows is best made when the forester checks the site and makes his recommendation on what to plant. Without this advice it is usually safe to compromise on a seven-foot spacing. Eight is often recommended for red pine, but one theory holds that this encourages rapidly tapering tree trunks with heavy side branches. Seven feet is the choice of this school of thought. White pine may be set five feet apart rather than the usually recommended six, on the theory that the closer spacing gives better protection from the white pine weevil. But the forester's experience and knowledge of local conditions are the best guide.

The number of seedlings per acre required for planting at various spacings is as follows:

SPACING	SEEDLINGS PER ACRE
5 x 5	1742
6 x 6	1210
7 x 7	889
8 x 8	680
10 x 10	436

Why so many trees crowded into an acre? Early mortality from any number of causes will dispose of some. More significantly, early crowding will encourage the growth of clear wood, free from knots. Crowding will tend to kill the lower branches and provide some natural pruning, to be supplemented later by human attention as the tree grows higher. The ultimate objective is 150 to 200 mature trees per acre for a final harvest.

If planting is to be done in the spring or early summer (the best time), it is well to check where, what, and how much with the forester during the preceding late summer or fall, before a snowfall.

Seedlings should be ordered at least three months in advance of planting time. The state forestry department nurseries are the best source, and the forester or county agent will provide details of ordering—but the supply goes to first comers, and late-season orders may find the supply has been exhausted.

The care of seedlings after delivery and during the planting operation is of paramount importance. They must be kept cool and moist until they go into the ground. They should be well watered as soon as they arrive. If there is to be some delay in planting, one suggestion is to dig a little ditch along the edge of a garden, then cover the roots well with loose soil and add water. Or wrap them in burlap or grain sacks and water. When planting, a fair supply can be carried along the rows in a bucket or basket—again, covered by moist earth. The main stock should be kept moist as circumstances permit.

One's own ingenuity must solve the problem of how to lay out a planting grid. The hope is that five or so years later the straight and evenly spaced rows will march across the field like a well-drilled regiment, every man in his place. A couple of balls of the cheapest white twine provided straight base lines for our only attempt at this with a seven-foot measuring stick to fix the intervals. A compass would have provided nicely exact right-angle corners, but this seemed a little over-precise at the time, so an old survey trick came to mind. Stand on the base line and extend the arms out to the side, arms and back lined up with the base line. Without moving the shoulders, bring the arms forward, put thumbs together, and sight over the thumbs. If there is a pocket tape handy, the resulting angle can be checked with the old three-four-five rule for the two sides and hypotenuse of a right triangle. Measure back three feet from the corner along the base line, and put in a twig marker. Next measure four feet along the line you hope is at a right angle to the base line and mark the point. Now five feet on the tape should join the three- and four-foot points, forming the long side of the right triangle. If not, move the four-foot line accordingly.

Passages to give easy access to the whole plantation are a great convenience if it is to be kept under cultivation. Inspection, pruning and thinning, and eventual harvest all involve movement of man and machine. If intensive cultivation is to be part of the program, plant three rows, then skip a row. The open space will do no harm, and may even benefit the growth. But these lanes will have to be watched for intrusive weed trees and kept open, lest the area they subtract from planting be worse than wasted.

One such case of neglect is a ten-acre red pine plantation on an excellent site. The owners were enthusiastic about using it as a demonstration plot, and welcomed the three-row layout. Fifteen years later it was a shambles of waist-high weeds and self-sown white pine, cherry, birch and poplar. The pine had been pruned once to six or eight feet and there were some fine young trees four to six inches in diameter, but many were crowded by this invading growth. Any improvement work such as a thinning for posts or pulp wood, or even the removal of invading weed trees, was going to be difficult, and expensive in time or money or both. In another five or ten years the sturdiest of the present trees can probably be harvested, but the plantation will have produced only a small fraction of its potential.

HOW TO PLANT SEEDLINGS

Planting seedlings is a relatively simple operation. The quickest method involves a team of two and a narrow spade. Number 1 drives the spade vertically into the ground and pushes the handle away from him. This makes a V-shaped hole. Number 2 places the seedling in the hole close to the vertical side, spreading the roots as he does so. The root collar— noticeable as the point on the seedling that indicates the top of the root growth—should be the point where the seedling stem emerges from the soil, just at ground level. Number 1 slips the spade out of the hole, not disturbing the seedling roots, and moves to the next site. Number 2 pushes the disturbed soil back in place, closing the hole, stamps on both sides of the slit to compact the soil somewhat and prevent air from getting at the roots, and moves on to join his partner.

A slower method, which is said to produce a higher survival rate, may be desirable if the ground is very dry, or if there is heavy sod. In this case a round-nose shovel may be used to advantage. First step is to scoop off a piece of sod at the planting site. Then a shovelful of soil is lifted out, and another from the opposite side to make a round hole. Seedling goes in, with well-spread roots, and dirt goes back in the hole. Seedling is held to keep the root collar at ground

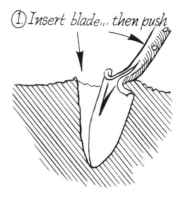

① Insert blade... then push

23. Planting a seedling.

level. More dirt goes in to fill the hole, then two or three stamps with the foot compact the fill to exclude air. *Important details:* avoid crowding the roots; position root collar at ground level for proper depth; compact soil firmly to wind up the operation.

Planting can be done with a mattock or with a special type of spade called a planting bar or dibble. Mattock technique is substantially the same as with a spade. The planting bar, however, requires three thrusts into the ground compared to the single stroke with the spade. The first thrust with the bar goes in at an angle, the handle held toward the user. Bar is then pushed forward to the vertical to make a V-shaped slot. Seedling goes in against the vertical side of the slot after the bar is withdrawn. Bar is moved back toward the planter about two inches, and pushed straight down. Handle is then pulled back so the blade will pivot forward to firm the soil at the bottom of the roots of the seedling just planted, then pushed

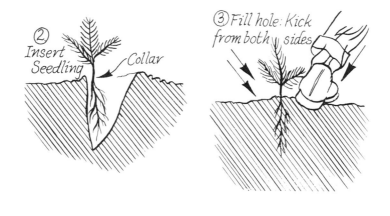

forward to close the top. This leaves another hole.
Bar moves back another two inches toward the
planter, goes in straight, then handle moves back and
forth to fill the hole. A kick with the heel packs down
this spot, then the soil around the seedling is packed
down. End of operation.

This rather more time-consuming procedure may
offer a theoretical advantage in compacting the soil
and protecting the roots. But a seedling, if it has been
properly cared for before planting, is a rugged individual whose survival rate is a matter of some
amazement for most amateurs. The tractor-drawn
planting machine is of course the fastest method—
and probably the only economical one—of planting
large areas. But there are few more satisfying re-
wards than the sight of straight-ranked young pines
and one's own private boast that "I planted you all
with my own two hands."

IX. Tools for the Woodlotter

ONE OF THE MOST satisfying aspects of woods work is the character of the tools employed. Generations of lumberjacks, tinkers and inventors have produced one tool after another, each perfectly designed for its purpose. The man who earns his living in the woods has no time to fool around with anything that fails to do a job well and quickly and with minimum physical effort. And the amateur woodlotter needs all the help he can get.

AXE AND SPLITTING HAMMER

The big, double-bitted axe of the old time lumberjacks, keen enough for the once-a-week shave as well as felling a tree, is almost an antique curio, as is the long, two-handled cross-cut saw. The modern chain saw now does their work. But a good axe is a must for any woodlotter. Though it may be used only infrequently, it should always be at hand to tap in a wedge when felling, when bucking a big log into fireplace lengths, or for lopping small limbs from a *felled* tree (but not for pruning a living tree). And of course there is no substitute for an axe if kindling is to be split.

We have found a relatively lightweight axe handier than a heavy one for most occasions. Our favorite lightweight has a twenty-four-inch handle and a two-pound head. This splits most of our kindling with minimum effort. A knotty or cross-grained piece gets the first lick with our slightly heavier two-and-a-half-pound model with a twenty-six-inch handle. A full-size axe has a three-and-a-half- to four-pound head and a twenty-eight- to thirty-two- or thirty-four-inch handle.

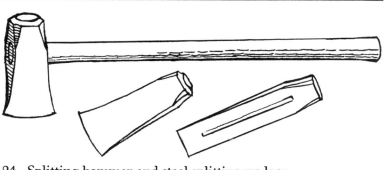

24. Splitting hammer and steel splitting wedges.

The axe is properly a cutting tool, not a hammer. When we suggest that even a light axe is handy to tap a wedge into place (when felling), the critical word is "tap," and such use should be further qualified in that the wedge should be hardwood or plastic, not steel. It is rank abuse of a good tool to drive a splitting wedge with an axe.

Driving a splitting wedge is properly the work of a maul or so-called *splitting hammer*. This may have a five-pound head and long handle, with a blunt cutting edge and a rounded poll like the head of a sledge hammer—of which it is of course a cousin, for their jobs are similar. One blow of the cutting edge may split a small billet into two pieces fireplace size if the wood is straight-grained and without big knots. Larger or unruly billets usually call for driving a splitting wedge to open a crack, after which another blow or two along the fracture will finish the job.

SHARPENING AN AXE

An axe, like any tool, deserves good care. As a cutting tool, it should be kept sharp, for safety's sake as well as efficiency. A dull axe is a dangerous axe, for instead of biting into the surface, a dull blade may glance off and strike the ground, or a leg or a foot. Frequent sharpening is thus a good habit—but there is more than meets the eye in this operation, since the shape of the cutting edge can contribute much to the efficiency of the blade.

For limbing and for use with softwoods a thin cutting edge is desirable. For hardwoods and for splitting, a wider angle is more appropriate. We have never been able to buy gauges to measure this difference, but from an illustration in a handbook we made a pair, using the stiff paper of an office file folder. With a pencil compass set to three-quarters of an inch we drew a short arc, then marked two points on the arc a quarter of an inch apart, and cut a notch from these two points to the center. This for the shape of our hardwood edge. For softwood, we repeated the process but set our two points three-sixteenths of an inch apart, thus making a narrower or thinner cutting edge for softer woods.

The wide face of a grindstone turned by hand is another relic of the past, supplanted by the electric bench grinder which does a fast cutting job, but whose speed is more than likely to heat the axe edge and spoil its temper. A flat file, the better for being slightly worn, is a safer sharpening tool. If a file is

---

25. How to make an axe-grinding gauge.

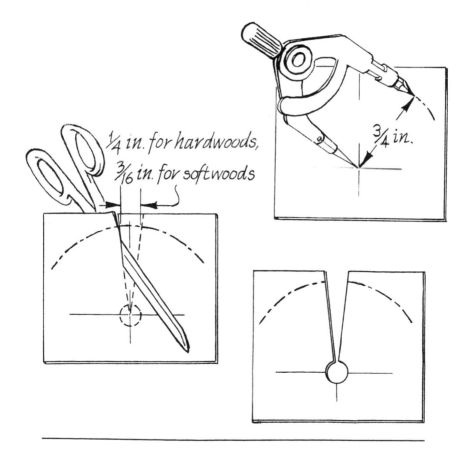

¼ in. for hardwoods,
³⁄₁₆ in. for softwoods

¾ in.

used, a good safety device is a small washer, made
from thin plywood or layers of heavy corrugated or
paper board, slipped over the handle, to keep one's
fingers away from the axe edge.

Filing is a relatively simple skill to master. The
trick is to make each stroke in the same plane to
produce a flat surface at the chosen angle to the edge.
After a stroke or two the fresh metal of the filed surface will reveal the angle at which the file is cutting
and the position of the file can be changed accordingly. Each stroke should then be made at the same
angle. With one hand on the file handle and the other
on the tip or front end, the stroke should be from
tip to handle, away from the body, and most important, with uniform pressure on both ends of the
file. After filing, the edge may be finished with a
whetstone to remove any burr left by the file.

BOW SAW

Though the axe has work to do and is worthy of
the best of care, its function has greatly diminished
since the days of the pioneer and the old-time logger.
The bow saw and the chain saw are by far the most
useful aids to the woodlotter. The chain saw now
does the work of felling, and with the bow saw com-
pletes the work of limbing. Then the chain saw
handles the job of bucking the tree into saw logs or
firewood lengths.

In many respects a small bow saw with sixteen- to
eighteen-inch blade is the handiest tool in the woods.
Razor sharp, it will fell a sapling or lop a limb in a

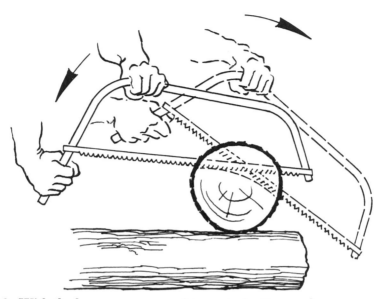

26. With the bow saw, use a rocking cut; don't press down.

few strokes, and is equally quick to trim off low branches when pruning. It is, of course, infinitely safer to use than axe or chain saw. One must have room to swing an axe, free from the obstruction of branch or twig that might deflect the blade, and both axe and chain saw demand a firm stance. This is particularly essential when using the chain saw, which is probably the most lethal instrument in the hand of man, demanding as it does complete control every second it is operating.

Not the least merit of the bow saw is the way it fits a woman's hand. It is my wife's principal and most efficient tool, and when it comes to lopping branches, pruning, or felling saplings up to four or five inches in diameter, she does a man's quota with the greatest of ease.

Our tool rack carries three of these little bow saws —no sign of affluence, for they are not expensive— and a new blade now and then is easier than finding and paying an expert to sharpen them. A couple of spare bow saws on hand can provide a subtle way of taking advantage of visitors or children who express a desire to "lend a hand" or "see what you do in the woods." Hand them a bow saw and the opportunity is theirs.

CHAIN SAW

Chain saws come in many sizes, from two-man monsters to a featherweight that can be managed with one hand. When the lightweights came on the market some years ago we were happy to shift from the first one we owned, then considered a small model but still weighing around thirty pounds, to the lightest of the new models. This has a sixteen-inch blade and weighs about fifteen pounds fully charged with gas and oil. An even lighter model developed a few years later with a twelve-inch blade weighs but ten pounds. The two make a perfect combination. The sixteen-inch blade will handle anything up to eighteen or twenty inches in diameter, and the smaller one is ideal for limbing, cutting firewood, and felling smaller trees.

There is much good natured argument among chain saw owners as to the "best" brand, but more

important than the brand, in our experience, is the
dealer who sells the saw. Saws will take a lot of abuse,
but an accommodating and expert dealer is a friend
indeed when repairs or service are needed.

If something goes wrong with the saw when working in the woods it is more than frustrating not to
know the machine well enough to make adjustments
or repairs on the spot. It is a good idea to include a
screwdriver and wrench with the reserve supply of

27. Readying the chain saw for action.

gasoline and oil at the work site, plus an allen wrench or any other special tool that may be needed. A new saw owner should of course take time, when the dealer delivers the saw, to read the owner's handbook then and there. And it is just as well to test his understanding by taking off the bar and chain, reassembling it, and readjusting the chain to the proper tension, all under the dealer's eye.

Spark plugs do not last indefinitely; a new plug is the easiest way to insure an easy-starting saw. The air filter must be kept reasonably clean with a periodic wash or blow-off with a high-pressure air hose. Keep the chain out of the dirt when sawing a log on the ground, and suspect any tree that has been used as a fence post of harboring wire or staples that will dull or damage the chain.

A bad plug is not always to blame for starting trouble. Too much choke may have flooded the motor. The cure in many cases is to turn the saw muffler-side down and return the choke to normal position, as when the motor is operating. Hold the throttle in full open position, pull the starter cord—and hope for the best. The operation may have to be repeated once or twice before the flooded motor will start.

We have never had the courage to sharpen our own saws, relying instead on the dealer's expert touch with file and gauge. The cutting tooth of the chain is a marvel of ingenious design, shaped like a half-round chisel with a special bevel to take out a sliver of wood with each pass. The depth of the cut and angle must be right, and this requires a good hand on the special file designed for this purpose.

For the more ambitious owner who would do his own chain sharpening, full details of the operation are usually found in the manual delivered with the new saw. The instructions will identify the correct size of the round file to be used, describe the file holder and its use, as well as the depth gauge required to control the bite of the cutting edge of the chain tooth. A more comprehensive manual on caring for the chain is a handbook of service and maintenance instructions supplied by Omark Industries, makers of the widely used Oregon brand of chain. This, too, can usually be supplied by the dealer when the saw is purchased.

As with any machine, good maintenance sustains good operation. The groove holding the chain in place on the bar should be cleaned periodically, and the cover plate over the sproket removed to get rid of accumulated grease and chips. Put a wrench on all nuts frequently to make sure they are snug. It is a good idea, too, to reverse the bar periodically to prevent undue wear. If it becomes difficult to draw the chain up to proper tension with the adjusting screw, let the dealer remove a chain link to shorten the chain.

The noise of a chain saw can be deafening. A report by the Surgeon General confirms this as fact. A set of ear muffs such as one sees on airport personnel working near jet planes eliminates this hazard— and also makes working with a chain saw a great deal more comfortable for the operator. They do not interfere with hearing even a normal conversation, but seem to filter out the high frequencies that can so seriously affect the ear. These noise suppressors can be purchased in most well-stocked gun shops and are also sold by the mail-order houses.

WEDGES

Wedges are as important a part of the woodlotter's tools as axe and saw. A wooden, plastic or aluminum felling or bucking wedge driven in behind the saw prevents the chain from binding, and will also force a tree to fall in the desired direction. A steel splitting wedge, as the name suggests, is used with a splitting hammer or maul to split a fireplace log, or, with one or more additional wedges, to split a longer log for posts or fence rails.

Felling or bucking wedges are made from any close grained hardwood such as rock maple, hornbeam, hickory, or even beech, as well as hard plastic, aluminum or magnesium. A steel wedge should never be used with a chain saw, for, as mentioned, just an instant's contact will ruin a chain. Dimensions may

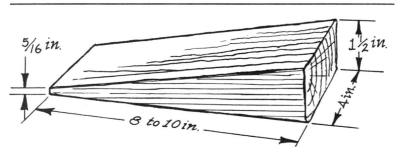

28. Typical wedge for use with a chain saw; it may be wooden, plastic or aluminum.

vary somewhat, but it is sometimes convenient to have two sizes, one somewhat larger than the other. The smaller may be three inches wide, six to nine inches long, and taper from ³⁄₁₆ or ¼ to 1½ inches. An eight- or ten-inch wedge might be four inches wide and taper from ⁵⁄₁₆ of an inch to 1½ or 2 inches at the head.

POLE SAW

Pruning requires a pole saw, or the special type of pole saw known as a Meylan saw—the latter somewhat more convenient and easy to work with because of the shape of its three-foot handle and the flat bracket attaching the sixteen-inch blade to the handle. Both types are made to have a convenient hook below the blade with which to free or pull down a pruned branch. The straight, round handle of the pole saw may be almost any length desired from six feet up, and supplants the Meylan for high pruning. The Meylan is handy if one is to fell an old pine whose low branches make it awkward to bring the chain saw to bear. With its long handle one can reach in to clear the base of the tree for easy access with the saw.

PEAVEY, PULP HOOK AND LOGGING CHAIN

A peavey is the logger's most useful tool. With it one can move a log about with ease. One wonders how logs could have been handled before Joseph

Peavey, a Maine blacksmith, invented it in 1858. *Peavey* and *cant hook* are terms sometimes used interchangeably, but the former has a sharp spike at the base, while the cant hook, though metal shod, has no point.

A pulp hook eases the work of handling four-foot lengths of pulpwood or in fact any short billet, even firewood logs.

---

29. The peavey.

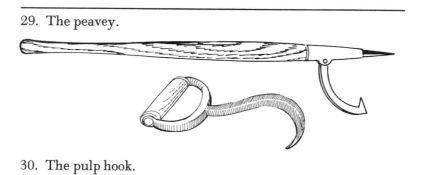

30. The pulp hook.

Nothing would move in the woods without the logging chain with a slip hook at one end and grab hook at the other. The slip hook, as the name suggests, permits the chain to slide through it and thus tighten its grip on whatever it is attached to. The grab hook fits snugly over a link to lock in place and stays put. Twelve- or fourteen-foot lengths are usual, but we find a twenty-four-footer with quarter-inch diameter links extremely useful and able to handle our needs as well as do the heavier ⅜-inch links of our other chains. The longer chain lives year round in the Jeep and its extra reach has been an asset on the highway as well as in the woods.

31. A slip hook.

A useful woodswise detail is proper use of the slip hook. This was pointed out to us one day by a farmer neighbor who watched with some amusement as our chain kept slipping off the log we were trying to move. "Turn your hook the other way," he finally suggested. It took a moment to think what he meant, but when we next hooked up, the back or closed part of the hook faced the direction of the pull. Our hook-ups thereafter stayed put.

X. Seasons & Seasoning

A MISCELLANY

WOODS WORK presents a diversity of tasks and the distaff side of a woodlotting couple can find much to do as Number Two (and sometimes as Number One) on a team with her husband. During the late spring and summer of garden time she is captain of the vegetable and flower command, but fall and winter release her from these almost daily responsibilities to join forces with me in the woods. There she plays a varied role, lending a hand in a shared enterprise that holds great satisfaction for both members of the team.

Handling a chain saw or wielding a splitting hammer are no woman's tasks, but there is much else to do, particularly in those operations where two sets of hands or heads are better than one. Often we have surveyed together the problems encountered in felling a big tree. What is the best direction for its fall? The chance of a clear fall without damage to other trees? The drift of wind? The delight of seeing careful plans pay off is enough to carry us through an occasional disappointment. Some trees just won't cooperate. Or we guess wrong and they hang up in the branches of a neighbor, to present additional intriguing problems. Two people to ponder may be no better than one, but there is companionship in mild disaster. A fine full-fledged hangup is less discouraging when two eye the problem, then go to work on it.

When all goes well in a chancy situation all credit
may go to Number Two. My wife and I planned to
thin a stand of small maples one day and had spent
quite a little time determining where we could drop
each one with a fair chance of a clear fall. We
wanted no hangups. But a gentle breeze was fast developing into a gusty wind as the chain saw was
readied for action. We watched the swaying tops and
debated whether to abandon our plans or take a
chance that we could outwit the wind. My wife took
station on a knoll where she could watch the tree
tops to the northwest where the wind was coming
from, as well as the trees we planned to cut. I made
the undercut on the first tree we had selected, then
just barely started the back cut and waited for her
signal to push the saw home. When the breeze died
between gusts and the tree stopped swaying, and
there was a quiet moment to the northwest as well,
Number Two gave the signal, the saw went home,
and the maple fell right on target. We felled five trees
that day with never a hangup.

In many other operations a partner plays a larger
part than the role of lookout. The sharp blade of the
little Swedish bow saw is her most effective tool for
cutting small-diameter weed trees or thinning over-
crowded young hardwoods. The same is true for pruning in the pines. Here my wife doubles the rate of
progress, taking the lower branches and moving on
while I follow with the longer handled Meylan saw
for the higher cuts. On occasion she backtracks to
join in stacking the fallen branches in windrows,
which leave clear passage among the trees and make

movement a great deal easier for future work or inspection tours.

Her bow saw goes into action again when tops and limbs must be freed from felled trees and stripped for later reduction to firewood. This is often some days after a hardwood is felled if buds or leaves are still on the branches, for these provide forage the deer never fail to nibble.

The ease with which a bow saw in a woman's skilled hand will go through a pine branch occasionally allows my wife to maneuver me into projects that are closer to her heart than mine. We had agreed that several big pines, random growth in the pastures, should be cleared out for aesthetic reasons. Cosmetic cutting, we call that. Number One thinks he has more important work to do, but the truth is he dislikes crawling in among big pine branches to get his saw into a tree. Somehow, these pines never seem to get on the work plan. But when Number Two and her bow saw get these annoying branches off, Number One is faced with a situation he can hardly ignore. The trees come down and Number Two scores her quiet triumph.

There are other areas in which roles are reversed and the distaff side becomes Number One. It is she who manages the young white birch fringing one of the pastures, thinning bit by bit as they develop, and weeding intrusive growth. Her enemy is the gaudy yellow-bellied sapsucker, who has drilled and girdled a number of promising trees. She vetoed a shotgun to eradicate the birds, for a new family would soon appear, and at any rate the trees they killed might well have to be thinned out as others matured.

We watched one day the performance of a pair raising a family in an old poplar. Their exhibition was well worth the loss of a tree or two. Father would fly to a big birch fifty feet from his hole in the poplar, take a ration for his young at one of the many holes he and his mate had drilled, and return to the nest hole. The instant he left the birch a humming bird arrived to snatch a drink where he had been working.

32. Sapsucker work on a young birch.

Then came Mother sapsucker for her ration, displacing the humming bird. Before Papa sapsucker returned a hovering moth or butterfly—we could not determine what—took a brief taste at the hole, only to fly off as the head of the family returned. This rotation continued with clocklike precision as we returned to our work of weeding young soft maples from the site.

One problem of the woodlotter's wife is worry about her husband's safety when working out of sight. If she can't hear the saw or the steady chink-chunk of the splitting axe or the sound of tractor pulling a log, she wonders what may have happened. She knows Number One is probably in less danger than on a through-way, but she worries just the same. The best solutions are the simplest. One is our habit of using a pair of shrill police whistles with which to communicate. If there is a long silence, blow the whistle. A responsive shrill will say, "All's well." More frequently if one partner needs a helping hand for some operation, two blasts, acknowledged, mean help is on the way.

We also make a practice of letting the left hand know what the right hand is doing, and where. When Number One goes off alone he may report, "Woodpile work near the sugar house down Forty-second Street. Back by four o'clock," or leave a note on the home post-board with a similar message. We are particularly careful to follow this practice in the winter, when low temperatures increase the hazards of long exposure. We are both sufficiently woods wise and winter wise to make safety a constant factor no matter what we are doing, but good communications have proved invaluable in relieving worry and increasing the pleasures we derive from our woodlotting.

Not the least of these pleasures for my wife is the satisfaction of a full woodshed. The neat stacks are reminders of days when she has made the foundation for a seasoning pile in the woods, stacked the short stovewood, then pitched it into the trailer for the trip home. She feels a special pride in the separate stack of sumac—the best of quick kindling—which she has harvested herself. Gratifying, too, is the end product of many a day's work when we have loaded the trailer with maple, ash, some hornbeam, and beech, brought it all out of the woods behind the Jeep and piece by piece arranged it along the woodshed walls. There will be twenty-two-inch split fireplace logs, a section of eight-inchers for the potbellied stove in the mud room, double that length for the kitchen–dining room parlor stove, and shorter ones for the bedroom fireplace. What wealth . . . one almost hates to burn it, but burn we do from mid-September to May. The sumac-quick blaze in the dining room takes off the chill at breakfast time nearly ten months of the year.

Winter is the most beautiful time in the woods, we believe. As cross-country skiers of long experience we are as often found roaming our own woods as exploring the well-nigh ideal terrain around us. Whether the hills are only dusted with snow or offer the icy crust that is the bane of all skiers, we find the woods equally inviting. Deep snow time is ideal for inspection trips on terrain where thick brambles make

summer maneuvering painful. When high pruning
is in order we wait for snow and crust to give us the
extra lift of a foot or two and leave the long-handled
and somewhat clumsy pole saw at home.

We move about on the snow much more quickly
on our skis than on foot, though we meet a good deal
of skepticism about this from believers in the tradi-
tion that snowshoes are the thing. Both skis and snowshoes have their place in woodlot work. It happens
that our working areas for the most part are on hillsides, some quite steep, at elevations of 1100 to 1350
feet. Entry from roadside to the pastures below the
woodland is at 970 feet, so we must climb a bit to do
our work, as well as cover from half a mile to more
than a mile of rolling terrain to reach our objectives.
Skis are thus most useful in saving time and energy
when our purpose is only to cruise an area, to pack in
tools or gas and oil for the saw, or to do some pruning.
Felling, bucking, or splitting and stacking firewood
must be done on foot. Ski boots are impossibly cold
for any extended work period on foot. It would indeed be a blessing if a ski-boot maker could be persuaded to produce an insulated model comparable to
the insulated and waterproof rubber or leather work
boot that is standard equipment for winter woods
work.

The only disagreement we have with our county
forester—an otherwise wholly admirable mentor—
is his reluctance to accept our ski doctrine. Skis come
off when felling or splitting and stacking firewood.
But we can add many minutes to the end of a beautiful afternoon when we are reluctant to leave the

woods. Our trip back to the Jeep at roadside takes no time compared with a return on foot or snowshoes.

Keeping warm in the woods in winter is no longer a problem since the advent of insulated boots and undergarments. The latter are not really necessary except for extreme conditions, but the insulated boot is a lifesaver. A felt insole is a good addition both for insulating quality and the convenience of removing the insole for thorough drying after being worn. For extreme conditions warmth is increased by first pulling on a pair of silk socks, then a moderate-weight woolen pair, and finally a so-called wick sock of special fabric that draws perspiration to this outside layer. It is best to buy these boots large enough to accommodate the sock layers, for a tight boot is a cold boot no matter what the sock combination.

For other seasons the best footwear is a leather boot that should provide the protection of a steel toe. The impact of a dropped wedge, a splitting hammer or a heavy log can inflict painful if not serious damage. These "safety boots" are not usually stocked by shoe departments, but most retailers will have the catalog of a work-boot manufacturer who can supply them on order. It is convenient to order a pair slightly larger than a street shoe to accommodate a heavy wool sock. Use a light insole to make the boot fit comfortably snug when weather calls for a lighter-weight sock.

A leather mitt (preferably deerskin for quick drying) is warmer than a glove for winter work when worn with a wool glove or mitten inside. The mitten will be the warmer combination. For maximum warmth, use two pairs of lightweight woolen mitts, and carry a spare in the pocket to replace the inner mitt if and when it becomes wet from the perspiration of one's hand.

Layers of lightweight outer garments are warmer than one heavy one. Two light wool sweaters over a workshirt, plus a windbreaker jacket are warmer than a heavy sweater. Discarding a sweater when one begins to perspire will preserve a comfortable balance.

Denim jeans are good for three seasons, but winter comfort calls for heavy wool—look for a thirty-ounce fabric—for real warmth. Working in prickly briers or in heavy brush is more comfortable when protected by "double front" pants—ten-ounce tight cotton fabric with an extra layer on front and sides from hip to ankle. For even more complete protection from waist to ankle, at least one forest workers' supply house offers heavyweight duck, slip-on chaps, to be worn like an overall.

All the gear for winter operations goes on an old toboggan which remains in the woods all season, covered with a heavy tarpaulin. With first snowfall, unless it is too deep for wheel travel, the Jeep drags toboggan, chain saws, peavey, axes and wedges up to a convenient headquarters. Gasoline, oil, and the maintenance kit are part of the load. Saws and other tools fit into slots and compartments in a stout wooden box screwed to the toboggan, which has a good length of rope for use when it is to be moved by hand to one or another work area. As an original ski patrolman, I long ago learned the practical impossibility of tow-

33. A toboggan carries all the gear.

ing a toboggan uphill on skis or even snowshoes. The trick is to pay out twenty or more feet of rope, take a stance with skis firmly across the slope, draw the toboggan up hand over hand, then take the rope end ahead and repeat.

"What a lot of work you must have done," is the comment we often hear from our visitors. "How long did it take to do your first ten acre plot, for example?" Our answers are usually wholly unsatisfactory. We might do bits and pieces over a period of eight or ten months, but we never punch a time clock. Our best answer is that we count our hours the way a canoeist on a long paddle will sometimes count his strokes, but forget the hundreds.

As a matter of fact, the casually maintained log of our operations shows that we reported ninety-eight hours for that first ten acres on the Agricultural Conservation Program form required to show completion of a project supervised by the county forester. Another entry shows forty-eight hours for a five-acre plot marked during the early winter and completed— all pruning and felling done and all felled trees lopped clean—by mid-March.

The first harvest of poplar, done one early May when we had to hurry to fell and peel the logs before the sap stopped running and peeling would be impractical, involved twenty hours during the course of six days. A note suggests that we achieved two cords to be made into excelsior at a nearby mill. One month of fine April weather we recorded twenty-seven hours in six days pruning and thinning red pine.

Truth of the matter is that we spend as much time in the woods as other duties and the weather permit. We limit the actual hours of physically demanding work to stay short of the fatigue point. Our work may or may not have some value, but we are working for pleasure, not a quota. Time runs but slowly in the woodlands and the condemned tree we fail to cut today can be felled as well next week or next month. There are few deadlines to meet and reasonable planning can accommodate them without driving one to long hours of what becomes toil.

The best time to work in the woods? There is really only one bad time—the black fly season of early spring. Mosquitos may be a bit of bother somewhat later in the year, but various ointments liberally applied minimize this nuisance. Nothing we have found, however, can cope with those tiny black flies, who are better left in undisputed possession for a time.

Winter is the best time to learn what creatures inhabit and move about the woods and fields. Tracks in the snow write the comings and goings for all to see. We learn that the deer have relished the last maple we felled, purposely leaving the top for their browse. They have attended to the last apples on the low branches, but will return again and again to the bare tree in the hope that something may have been overlooked. Our fox—or is it a visitor? For we do not always find the lair—writes a characteristic trail with one foot so exactly in front of another.

A visiting naturalist one day commented that our hardwood area with its clean forest floor and freedom from underbrush was a desert for wildlife. We were indignant. Desert, indeed. . . . Our woodpiles, covered with a sheet of corrugated metal roofing or heavy, tarred building paper, are condominiums for families of mice and chipmunks. Our border collie never tires of her games of hide and seek with the chipmunks.

One season, before the dog joined the family, we were puzzled by the faintest scent of musk as we worked up a stack of firewood. Can't be a skunk hereabouts, we thought. Nor was it skunk, for one bright day, looking up from our work, we saw a vixen not a hundred yards away keeping an eye on our operations. She repeated this for several days, sitting on her haunches apparently unworried by our presence.

Another vixen some years later was less compla-
cent, for by that time our dog was on the scene. We
were starting work at a new site and the dog had
gone off to check up on the territory. Suddenly a
series of banshee-like screeches came from beyond a
ridge—wild screams the like of which we had never
heard before. A moment later the collie came trotting
toward us, followed by a furious vixen yelling her
head off. The dog was obviously as surprised as we
that this furious little creature could produce such an
ear-splitting uproar. She was definitely getting the
message to "keep out of here."

Mice are the most accomplished opportunists in
setting up housekeeping. Mighty Mouse, our little
tractor, spends most of its life in the woodlot, covered
by an all-enveloping tarpaulin. We are never sure,
when we pull off the tarp after the machine has been
idle for some time, that we will not find a family of
mice comfortably established on the seat.

One early spring, after Mighty had been just a
small white mound under the heavy snow, I pulled
the tarpaulin off and began to wind the starting cord
to give the motor a turn or two. But by my hand there
appeared a little pink nose and a pair of beady eyes,
peering from behind the steel wire mesh protecting
flywheel and magneto. There is a favorite line in
Alice in Wonderland: "I told you butter wouldn't suit
the works." I thought of that as I waited for what
must have been at least two large families to evacuate
their homestead. The operating instructions for the
motor had not referred to the effect of mice meat on

the ignition. It was over an hour later that the last of the children had been persuaded to leave that nest. I am not sure that my need was greater than theirs, but conscience was appeased by the assumption that they would quickly find acceptable new quarters in a nearby wood pile.

RECOGNIZING TREES

We speak glibly of ash, beech, maple and other trees, but how does the amateur woodlotter recognize them? The best teacher, of course, is the forester. On his first cruise through the woodland or later when marking trees for improvement cutting, a steady flow of questions will produce not only identification but often some additional comment on the character and value of the species. He expects questions, for his far-from-minor objective is to teach.

"What's that tree?" one asks. "White ash." Five minutes later one touches a similar looking tree and says, "White ash?" "Good guess," says the guide. But next time, with more confidence, one says, "Nice looking ash there," and the reply is "No, that's a basswood."

"But the bark looks just like the one you said was ash."

"Well, almost," he will admit. But he will point high up to the basswood's fat leaves. "There's your sign—the big leaf. And look at the ash over there. See the way the twigs grow in pairs opposite each other on a branch. And the ash leaf has an entirely different shape."

Ash and basswood are problem trees because of this similarity of the bark. Even the forester will admit that winter identification is tricky when leaf shape gives no help. Basswood and ash are compatible neighbors and their branches may be so intermingled that it is difficult to determine which branch belongs to which tree.

A pair of bird-watching glasses to provide a close-up view of high branches is a great help in this identification game in any season, but particularly when the trees are bare.

Another device we have found useful is a small file card thumbtacked to a tree when first identified. Such a card, marked "ash" or "basswood," can be a useful reminder and will survive wind and weather long enough to serve its purpose.

If Number Two had used glasses in our early days in the woodlot, she would have saved face for Number One who had felled a tree and cut and split a fine harvest of fence posts from its logs. A neighbor was helping us run a line of fence to keep heifers out of the woods. "Need more posts," he had said. When Number One proudly produced his handiwork our friend said, "What are you going to do with those?" That ash turned out to be a basswood, and no fit material for a fence post.

Birch is easiest to name because of its whitish bark, but it may be any one of several kinds. We are told that birch has so many hybrids that even the professionals find it difficult to apply the right label. These include gray, paper, river, sweet, and yellow birch. Yellow birch is obvious because of its distinctive yellow or brownish-yellow color.

Beech has its own distinctive silver gray and relatively smooth-textured bark. The gray bark of an oak needs the characteristic shape of the leaf to make one sure of his guess. The bark of cherry, butternut and poplar are relatively easy to remember and recognize. (Poplar also carries the colloquial name of *popple*.)

The foregoing are all listed among the broad-leaved species. The needle-leaved species, loosely referred to as softwoods, are primarily identified by the number and character of their needles. Easiest to note are the five-needle cluster of white pine and the two needles of red pine.

The most complete guide to tree identification we have seen is the booklet by Reginald D. Forbes, "Woodlands for Profit and Pleasure," published by the American Forestry Association, 1319 18th Street, Washington, 20036, and available through the Association at $5.00 a copy, postpaid. It is an inclusive handbook full of practical information for the layman woodlot owner. *Trees of North America—A Guide to Field Identification* is another excellent handbook, published in paperback by Golden Press in their field guide series. Full color illustrations are particularly useful.

As an indication of how tricky tree identification can be from bark alone, look at the next page and try your hand at identifying these familiar species on the line below each photograph. Then turn to pages 152-157 to find them reproduced again (together with other species), this time with their proper names. It's a little easier in the field.

XI. On Buying a Woodlot

"WHERE CAN WE FIND a woodlot? What should we look for? How big? How do we find out?" These questions become more frequent as growing numbers of families seek escape from the city. Usually acquiring a woodlot is only a part of the larger objective of buying a place in the country. This may be a year-round home or an occasional temporary retreat. At any rate, advertisements extolling "forty wooded acres, brook, and comfortable spacious home" appear more frequently than "twenty acres of forest, brook, and view."

Simply finding a woodlot is no problem. Finding the *right* one is the rub. There are more real-estate brokers in "vacation home country" than one can shake a stick at. And so many offerings that many a seeker for the perfect thing may become as bewildered as one friend who remarked in disgust, "I feel like a dog chasing his tail."

A leisurely search extending perhaps over several seasons is likely to increase the chance of finding just the right landscape to call one's own. The most successful acquisitions in our experience have come just this way, to families who have spent enough time in a locality to learn its byways and some of its people. The land they found might not have been on a broker's list at the time. But in the course of exploring the countryside, those particular wooded hills had an immediate attraction. A tactful approach to the owner, arranged by a bit of diplomatic maneuvering to make his acquaintance, laid the groundwork for the sale.

More commonly the woodlot is only incidental to the purchase of a country home. The wooded land is valued only in terms of a setting for the dwelling—as part of the surrounding "scenery"—or as a shield to insure quiet and privacy. The new owners may relish the thought of cutting their own firewood, or perhaps look forward to plucking the Christmas tree from their own land, but many a property is purchased without more than a casual recognition that it included "some woods."

If woodland is in fact a major consideration, the most important question is "what do we want to do with a woodlot." Roam about in the woods, maybe camp out with the children, just enjoy it as a recreation area? How large the woodlot should be is a secondary consideration. Five acres to a hundred or more will serve.

But the greatest enjoyment and satisfaction in a woodlot lie in the meaningful work one can do for it. This means more than cutting firewood now and then to salvage something useful from a dead or dying tree. A new woodlot owner becomes trustee and keeper of a complex living organism subject to ills, decay and death but rewardingly responsive to knowledgeable care. Estimating the extent of one's involvement requires some thought, for there may be much to do.

To "hire the work done," as they say in our neighborhood, is no great problem. The county forester or a private consulting forester can assume practical management and direction of a program appropriate to the area. The private forester can engage men to do the necessary work under his supervision, subject to the owner's approval of the overall program, which the forester will develop for both short-term and long-term objectives.

A do-it-yourself program, on the other hand, is likely to yield the best return on a woodlot investment in terms of personal satisfaction and enjoyment. The critical factor here, however, is an honest assessment of both temperament and physical condition. This requires critical and impertinent questions. Do you really like being in the woods, or is this a romantic aspiration without much foundation in practical experience? Are you reasonably active physically? Woodlotting does not demand a lot of muscle, but it does provide plenty of exercise. Age is not a handicap if one is still playing tennis, skiing, or hiking. One virtue of woodlotting as an avocation is that it can be done bit by bit. One can tackle a thinning job with the intention to cover two or three acres in the course of a day. But half these acres can wait until tomorrow or next week. There is no compulsion to spoil the pleasure of a day in the woods by wearing one's self out in overambition.

The size of a woodlot is not, as previously pointed out, necessarily critical. There is occupation to be found in five or ten acres—depending, of course, on what they contain. A hundred acres is not too big to handle, and the larger area will add the interest of

greater variety than one is likely to find in a small
tract. There is no rule that a woodlot be all in one
piece. A village home or a country residence with
only a few acres of woodland can be supplemented by
several smaller tracts or a large one located within
reasonable distance. Several of our neighbors own and
work in areas some distance from our village, and we
have found it no handicap that ours is three and a
half miles from our home.

All the land need not be wooded. If soil and site are
appropriate a new pine plantation can be established
to return abandoned or worn-out pastures to productive use. Open fields, too, contribute much to the
quality of a landscape, framing the woods and perhaps offering the accent of free-standing trees that
have developed the full beauty of their natural form.

Open land imposes its own responsibilities for care.
Brush and tree growth from the woods invade its
borders and weeds appear everywhere. Keeping open
land open is sometimes a problem. Grazing controls
weed growth to some extent, but only sheep will crop
clean. If grass and water are adequate, a neighboring
farmer may be willing to put in some of his heifers. If
circumstances make it possible to provide for the necessary attention, the owner may want to acquire and
pasture his own catle. If the land is to be grazed, there
must be good fencing to keep cattle out of the woods
as well as on their own turf. Old pastures are likely to
have been fenced and little or no new wire may be
needed, but fence posts are another matter.

Old hay land can be restored at the cost of fertilizer
and cultivation. Soil samples will indicate the treat-

34. Spring snow—and a sunny day to prune.

ment. But hay must be mowed and this calls for time and machinery. Lacking both, the work can be "hired out" but is likely to be done only after everyone else has brought in his own hay crop. Hay cultivation or pasturing are not the only solutions to keeping the land in good condition. Annual clipping with a rotary or flail mower leaves a mulch to hold moisture and some nourishment, and with periodic use of lime can produce an attractive cover of natural grass.

What should one seek in a woodlot? Ideally, look for a bit of everything. Diversified species will provide a variety of activities. Pines will call for periodic pruning and thinning and if the trees are self-seeded their

random growth will pose intriguing problems of release cutting. Hardwoods will not be pruned but need
other attention and will of course supply firewood.
The faster-growing pine will produce earlier cuttings for income such as posts or pulpwood if the
acreage is large enough to give adequate volume.
Open land adjacent to the woodlot may be appropriate
for planting red or white pine.

Much of the pleasure of woodlot work lies in the eye
of the beholder. There is little need to warn against
purchase of cut-over land on which careless logging
has left a jungle of dead tops and high stumps. These
will eventually disappear but the area will hold no
promise for years. Nor is there much reward in a
hardwood lot in which mature trees have not been
harvested but allowed to decay from over-age and in
which, for one reason or another, no new growth has
taken place for the future.

An intermixture of birch and the dark green of the
conifers with which they are compatible makes a
pattern to please the eye, but birch is a relatively
short-lived tree, subject to damage by storm and snow,
and to the destructive appetite of the yellow-bellied
sapsucker. A good stocking of poplar is not a liability
if there is a nearby market for posts or other cuttings.
It is fast growing and relatively short-lived, but not
easily eradicated, as we once learned.

Our lesson came from a dense growth of poplar
bordering the sidehill road up to our woodlot. A few
good-sized trees were dying and beginning to shed
their branches. The rest was a jungle of young trees.
We had not yet consulted the forester who was to

guide us later in our first planned weeding and thinning operations, but we thought poplar was a weed tree and might as well be shot on sight. This jungle should be given a thorough cleaning, we said. Our eager-beaver attack with chain saw and bow saw eliminated all but a few straight young trees and we felt great satisfaction in the improved appearance of the landscape after several days of work. A few years later new growth had appeared on our well-scrubbed site. These saplings, dense as before, had largely re-created the jungle we had so proudly eliminated. But by then we had learned that our poplar was readily marketable and had in fact made a number of sales to a nearby user. This new growth, needless to say, is now receiving the same care as the rest of the woodlot and it will not be long before it will yield a useful crop.

Taxes and inflated land values are such that forest land must be near the bottom rank of investments for income. Potential appreciation, quite aside from the values of its timber, is another matter depending on elements too numerous and diverse to discuss here. A woodlot may well supply enough lumber for a house or barn, as our neighbors have demonstrated. One had enough pine for a new cow barn; another— a do-it-yourself woodlotter on a large and intensive management scale—drew enough big logs to a mill to provide beautiful wide boards for all the flooring in a new village home. A woodlot is for pleasure and profit too, but immediate profit should perhaps be considered in things of the spirit rather than an entry on the tax form.

The best way to confirm one's judgment in the choice of a woodlot is a walk through the area with a consulting forester. This will reveal just what it holds, identify the species and suggest the character of the work to be done. A major consideration will be his recognition of the owner's plans and ambitions. Today's forester recognizes many factors largely subordinated in the past, when his objective was the most economical way to produce a sustained yield of good timber. He is now willing to consider something more than maximum board feet and to recognize the aesthetic inclinations of his clients.

An illustration of this change of heart is a stand of hemlock along a brook in our own woodlot. On his first tour through this area, marking the adjoining hardwoods for improvement cutting, we suggested pruning these hemlocks. "No value to that," he said. "They are too large to prune now and you won't add to their value by doing it. Don't bother."

But prune we did. Number Two with her little bow saw and longer pole saw cleared all lower branches to seven or eight feet. We now have one of the most beautiful brooksides, a pleasure to walk or ski through at any season.

A brook and pond are assets to grace a contemplated piece of land. If a pond is lacking, a bulldozer can create a small one in a few days' time. Ours required only two days. Finishing touches with rake and shovel occupied two more, after which my wife took charge of planting. Wild flag, iris, daffodils and lilies have thriven around its borders with a minimum of attention. Lawn seed, fertilizer and a half hour's work with the home lawn mower now and then have created a grassy enclave for lazing about on hot summer days. Here the children played for hours until they outgrew the fascination of salamanders, polliwogs and frogs. Then a few brown trout were introduced to reduce this population and to test the skill of one grandchild who was becoming a fisherman.

Access is an important consideration in a woodlot purchase. There is little virtue in a woodlot that is inaccessible on many a day which may be perfect for working up firewood or felling a condemned tree or two. What appears to be a satisfactory dirt road leading to the woodlot may be all but impassable in spring mud season. Snow may block the way. The broker's assurance that this is a town road with year-round maintenance is no guarantee. Who lives on the road and must use it in all weathers? Are there children who must get to school despite mud and snow? Discreet inquiry, or even a talk with the town road foreman, may be revealing.

When the decision to buy has been made, the most important detail by far is the precise location of your property lines. Country deeds are notoriously casual. "Beginning at the elm tree marking the northeast corner the property extends northerly to John Jones's pasture, thence easterly et cetera." The elm (which elm?) may long since have succumbed to age and the elm bark beetle. The pasture may be overgrown and its limits no longer discernible.

There is one best way to resolve these uncertainties. Walk the boundaries with the owner and your neighbors-to-be. Identify and mark the corners. In cases of uncertainty, make adjustments and secure the agreement that your neighbor will execute quitclaim deeds to confirm the new property lines.

Properties are sometimes described as "fifty acres, be it more or less," and the area may indeed be considerably more or less. A survey is always desirable and sometimes essential to fix the area and define boundaries. The surveyor will confirm the truth of the saying "good fences make good neighbors" but will add that well-marked boundaries are even more important than fences. He will certainly suggest marking corners with something visible and permanent. A length of iron pipe with a coat of red rust-resistant paint is a good choice. Boundary lines, too, should be well marked, and at frequent intervals. A thick splash of bright paint—yellow is often the choice—on trees along the line will last several years.

Metal discs are a good alternative to paint, which we abandoned after one tiresome and time-consuming trial run. We cut out and saved tops and bottoms of the larger-size tin cans. When we had accumulated a good supply we dunked them in a can of anti-rust paint. These were easy to tack to trees, arm's-length high overhead. We used galvanized roofing nails which have a large head, but avoided driving the nail all the way, leaving a small gap under the head for a hammer or pry bar to remove the nail if and when it might later be necessary to fell the tree (for of course nails and chain saw do not mix). These markers, high enough to be clearly visible, seem as good as new after nearly ten years' exposure.

Glossary of Terms
and Units of Measure

Acre. 43,560 square feet; 4840 square yards; 160 square rods; 10 square chains. A one-acre square has sides of 208.7-plus feet.

Billet. A short round section of log.

Board Foot (BF). A unit of wood measure 12 inches square by 1 inch thick.

Bolt. A short (to 5 ft.) section of wood. A bolt of pulpwood.

BTU (British thermal unit). The heat required to raise one pound of water through one degree Fahrenheit.

Buck. To cut a log to desired length.

Chain. 4 rods; 66 feet.

Cord. 128 cubic feet—a woodpile 4 x 4 x 8 feet. *Face Cord.* A 4 x 8 ft. pile of wood pieces shorter than 4 ft. pieces. A 4 x 8 ft. pile of 24-inch wood is thus one-half cord. NOTE: The net volume of wood in a cord is approximately 90 cubic feet.

Crop tree. Tree capable of yielding one or more saw logs, or having saw log potential and thus reserved for harvesting.

DBH (Diameter Breast High). Point 4½ feet from ground at which to measure diameter of a standing tree as a basis for determining the number of board feet a log will yield.

Fell. To cut down a tree.

Log Rule. Log Scale. A "yardstick" 30 inches long, calibrated to show the board feet contained in logs 8, 10, 11, 12, 14, 16 feet long.*

Lop. To cut off. To remove limbs from a felled tree.

Rod. 16½ feet.

Saw log. A log suitable for sawing into lumber.

Scale. To measure board feet. ("The log scaled 60 bf.")

Section. 1 square mile. 640 acres.

Skid. To drag a log along the ground.

Stem. A tree. The tree trunk. The portion of a tree below the
lowest branch.

Sweep. The natural bend in a log. A long gentle bend.

Top. Top portion of a tree, too small for a saw log; includes both
stem and limbs.

Yard. Place where logs are accumulated.

To Translate Circumference to Diameter

Circumference		Diameter		Circumference		Diameter	
12½	inches	4 inches		44	inches	14 inches	
18¾	"	6	"	47⅛	"	15	"
25⅛	"	8	"	50¼	"	16	"
31⅜	"	10	"	53⅜	"	17	"
37¹¹⁄₁₆	"	12	"	56½	"	18	"
40⅞	"	13	"				

* Log rules (pp. 53 and 59) are sometimes hard to find. If your local hard-
ware store doesn't have one, try: Forestry Suppliers, Inc., Box 8397, Jackson,
Mississippi 39204; The Bon Meadows Co., 553 Amsterdam Avenue, Atlanta,
Georgia 30306; or The University Bookstore, University of Maine, Orono,
Maine 04473.

Suggested Reading

There are apparently few books on forestry for the general reader, despite a wealth of texts and studies for the student and the professional. The following works, however, are readily available and offer much useful basic information for the amateur.

"Logging Farm Wood Crops" (Farmers' Bulletin No. 2090, U.S. Dept. of Agriculture)

"Managing the Family Forest" (Farmers' Bulletin 2187, U.S. Dept. of Agriculture)

(Both of the above pamphlets are available from: Superintendent of Documents, U.S. Government Printing Office, Washington, D.C. 20250, 20 cents each.)

"Why T.S.I.: Timber Stand Improvement Increases Profits" (U.S. Forest Service PA–901; Dept. of Agriculture, Washington, D.C. 20250)

Woodlands for Profit and Pleasure, Reginald D. Forbes (The American Forestry Association, 1319 18th Street, Washington, D.C. 20036, $5.00 postpaid.)

Cherry   Ash

Basswood   Maple

Maple—old growth   Beech

Hop hornbeam (remmen)   Butternut

White birch

Hemlock

Locust

Poplar

White pine

Red pine

Ash—young tree

Yellow birch

Oak—young tree   Oak—large tree

Elm—young tree   Elm—large tree

Index

References to illustrations are printed in italic.